KOREAN
VEGETARIAN

KOREAN
VEGETARIAN

EXPLORE THE SPICY AND ROBUST TASTES OF A CLASSIC CUISINE,

WITH 55 RECIPES SHOWN IN 300 STEP-BY-STEP PHOTOGRAPHS

YOUNG JIN SONG

southwater

This edition is published by Southwater, an imprint of Anness Publishing Ltd, Blaby Road, Wigston, Leicestershire LE18 4SE
Email: info@anness.com

www.southwaterbooks.com; www.annesspublishing.com

If you like the images in this book and would like to investigate using them for publishing, promotions or advertising, please visit our website www.practicalpictures.com for more information.

ETHICAL TRADING POLICY

At Anness Publishing we believe that business should be conducted in an ethical and ecologically sustainable way, with respect for the environment and a proper regard to the replacement of the natural resources we employ.

As a publisher, we use a lot of wood pulp to make high-quality paper for printing, and that wood commonly comes from spruce trees. We are therefore currently growing more than 750,000 trees in three Scottish forest plantations: Berrymoss (130 hectares/320 acres), West Touxhill (125 hectares/305 acres) and Deveron Forest (75 hectares/185 acres). The forests we manage contain more than 3.5 times the number of trees employed each year in making paper for the books we manufacture.

Because of this ongoing ecological investment programme, you, as our customer, can have the pleasure and reassurance of knowing that a tree is being cultivated on your behalf to naturally replace the materials used to make the book you are holding.

Our forestry programme is run in accordance with the UK Woodland Assurance Scheme (UKWAS) and will be certified by the internationally recognized Forest Stewardship Council (FSC). The FSC is a non-government organization dedicated to promoting responsible management of the world's forests. Certification ensures forests are managed in an environmentally sustainable and socially responsible way.
For further information about this scheme, go to www.annesspublishing.com/trees

Publisher: Joanna Lorenz
Project Editors: Emma Clegg and
    Hannah Consterdine
Introduction text: Young Jin Song and Catherine Best
Photographer: Martin Brigdale
Home Economist: Lucy McKelvie
Stylist: Helen Trent
Designers: Tony Cohen and E-digital Design
Illustrator: Rob Highton
Production Controller: Bessie Bai

PUBLISHER'S NOTE
Although the advice and information in this book are believed to be accurate and true at the time of going to press, neither the authors nor the publisher can accept any legal responsibility or liability for any errors or omissions that may be made.

Previously published as part of a larger volume, *The Complete Book of Korean Cooking*.

NOTES
Bracketed terms are intended for American readers. For all recipes, quantities are given in both metric and imperial measures and, where appropriate, in standard cups and spoons. Follow one set of measures, but not a mixture, because they are not interchangeable.

Standard spoon and cup measures are level. 1 tsp = 5ml, 1 tbsp = 15ml, 1 cup = 250ml/8fl oz.
Australian standard tablespoons are 20ml. Australian readers should use 3 tsp in place of 1 tbsp for measuring small quantities.

American pints are 16fl oz/2 cups. American readers should use 20fl oz/2.5 cups in place of 1 pint when measuring liquids.

Electric oven temperatures in this book are for conventional ovens. When using a fan oven, the temperature will probably need to be reduced by about 10–20°C/20–40°F. Since ovens vary, you should check with your manufacturer's instruction book for guidance.

The nutritional analysis given for each recipe is calculated per portion (i.e. serving or item), unless otherwise stated. If the recipe gives a range, such as Serves 4–6, then the nutritional analysis will be for the smaller portion size, i.e. 6 servings. Measurements for sodium do not include salt added to taste. Medium (US large) eggs are used unless otherwise stated.

Contents

INTRODUCTION

In this introduction we explore the geography, climate and landscape of

both North and South Korea, looking at the historical influences that have

shaped the countries themselves and subsequently the cuisine that has become

so popular around the world today. The book then moves on to the countries'

vegetarian cuisine, culinary traditions, cooking methods and the ingredients that

can be found in a Korean menu. Finally, there are introductory recipes for some

of the essential flavours of Korean cooking.

GEOGRAPHY, CLIMATE & LANDSCAPE

The countries of North and South Korea form an area of vibrant contrasts. They embrace light-filled bustling modern cities, natural landscapes seemingly unchanged over centuries, and traditional cultures developed over time. The geography and seasonal changes dictate how to work the land, and farmers grow a mixture of arable crops, rice and cattle wherever the mountainous terrain flattens out enough to be tilled. The diversity of Korea also unfolds within the country's eating traditions, showing the influence of Buddhism and Confucianism, the use of seasonal local ingredients and the culture of sharing multiple dishes.

NORTH AND SOUTH

The two countries are deeply divided between the Communist North and the democratic South. It is difficult for outsiders to obtain much information about everyday life in North Korea; but from what we understand about the country, the people live in a relatively restricted fashion, a real contrast to life in bustling, prosperous South Korea. However, longstanding Korean food and farming traditions persist throughout the country, with fresh and natural ingredients grown or fished locally in what is a productive, industrious land.

THE LANDSCAPE OF KOREA

The small Korean peninsula, a spit of land pushing into the sea, is joined to the mainland only on its northern edge, where it touches the giant land masses of China and Russia. A tiny stretch of the border, only 19km (12 miles) long, skims the southern edges of Siberia just south of Vladivostok. The remainder of the border follows the winding courses of two rivers for 1,400km (880 miles) to

Above: A young farmer surveying the landscape near Kyongju, South Korea. Cultivating the land provides many of the major ingredients essential to Korean cooking.

separate Korea from the ancient land of Manchuria, now known as China. The eastern side of the country is protected from the Pacific Ocean by the curving islands of Japan. The enmity between these two countries over many centuries is underlined by the fact that the Koreans now prefer to call the stretch of water which divides them the East Sea, rather than the older name, the Sea of Japan.

Korea has a rich variety of natural fauna and flora, from the native broad-leaved trees of the south of the country, which flourish in the humid climate, to spikier pine trees, larch and juniper in the colder north. Luckily, there are no active volcanoes in Korea, but a number of hot springs mean that the earth is quietly rumbling not far below the surface, and small earthquakes are common.

Left: Farmworkers picking tea leaves in Boseong, South Korea, famous for its green tea leaves. If leaves are picked before 20 April, they are thought to be of the very best quality.

THE KOREAN CLIMATE

The terrain is both rugged and beautiful, and the climate comprises similar harsh extremes: blazing heat in the humid summer and snow in the icy winter. The southern regions have a similar climate to that of Japan, with warm, wet summers and a regular monsoon season which brings half the year's rainfall in a few weeks. Farther north, it is much drier and colder, with snow on the mountains and freezing temperatures in winter.

COUNTRY LIFE

Korea is described as the Land of Morning Calm, and outside the cities, this is clearly borne out by cloud-enshrouded mountains dominating the landscape, blanketed by lush meadows and dotted with picturesque villages. Working monasteries open their doors, and the friendly locals welcome travellers enthusiastically, happy to share their meals with interested tourists.

The farmers of Korea do, however, have a challenging brief against the twin limitations of mountainous terrain and encroaching cities. On every square metre of level ground you will find either buildings or agriculture. Where there is room for farming, they raise animals for meat – beef and pork being the most popular meat in Korea – or grow rice, which fills over half the fields of Korea and forms the delicious, glutinous base of every Korean meal. Where other crops are grown, they are usually barley, wheat and corn to mill into flour for pancakes and fritters, or a great variety of delicious vegetables and fruit.

Above: The dramatic Kumgang mountains in North Korea are located on the east coast, just above the north/south country border.

CITY LIFE

Korea is a fascinating blend of the fiercely traditional and the breathtakingly modern. The great cities are like neon tigers, with skyscrapers soaring into the air. Seoul's lights shimmer and sparkle, reflected in the waters of the Han River, and everywhere there is a vibrant sense of a thriving, prosperous, 21st-century society. There has been a general drift of the country's population to the big cities of South Korea, several of which have more than a million inhabitants packed tightly into a small area. Most of these people live in 20-storey high-rise blocks of apartments, which resemble each other so closely that they often have ornate murals painted on the side to differentiate one block from the next.

Some Koreans still live in a traditional way even in the big cities, though many younger people now embrace a Western way of life and most learn English with an eye to their future prosperity. However, the family remains an important part of life, and Koreans generally show great respect for older people in society.

Korea's main cities

Seoul (South Korea)
A pulsating 21st-century city of towering skylines and ancient temples, with a thriving nightlife.

Busan (South Korea)
The largest port in Korea, built on the south-eastern coast facing Japan.

Pyongyang (North Korea)
Generally rebuilt since the Korean War, with many monuments and huge buildings.

Daegu (South Korea)
Inland city and centre of a web of transport networks, built at the junction of two rivers centuries ago.

Left: A typical Korean village surrounded by rice fields. Rural life centres on the village, and is based on the mutual solidarity of the inhabitants.

HISTORICAL INFLUENCES

Korea has always been a crossroads of cultures, absorbing the influences of the surrounding countries while developing a distinct national identity.

From the middle of the 1st century BC Korea began to develop as a recognizable country. This was the beginning of the era of the Three Kingdoms: Koguryo, Paekje and Silla. The kingdoms fought among themselves for dominance until the end of the 7th century, when Silla defeated the other two, with Chinese aid, and unified the peninsula under central rule.

MONGOLIAN AND CHINESE INFLUENCE

The southern migration of Mongolian tribes to Korea in the 1st century BC from Manchuria (now China) brought great changes, in cultural and agricultural terms. The shamanistic beliefs of the Mongols were adopted by the Koreans, as were their cultivation techniques. The Mongols taught the Korean people how to farm the plains, raise cattle and grow crops, and this influenced the country's cuisine, which then started to move away from a predominantly seafood-based diet.

The origins of the Korean tofu and vegetable casserole *chungol* can be traced back to Mongolia. The Koreans adapted the recipes of migrating Mongol tribes from the north, using local

ingredients to produce regional variations in which the flavours were carefully matched to accompanying dishes.

THE INFLUENCE OF BUDDHISM

At the end of the 7th century Korea entered a long stable period based on Buddhist culture. This had a great effect on the nation's gastronomy, as the slaughtering of animals was prohibited under Buddhist principles.

Diets changed with this dramatic reduction in the consumption of meat,

Above: The influence of Buddhism in Korea led to the elevated importance of vegetables, over meat, in Korean food.

and vegetables took on a much more significant role. Temple meals consisted of soup, rice and vegetable dishes, and omitted strong-smelling ingredients, such as garlic or spring onions (scallions). This influence is still apparent in the *namul* vegetable dishes of modern Korea, and the technique of marinating in soy sauce, rice vinegar and sesame seeds has barely changed. Interestingly, the simple porridge and vegetable dishes of the Buddhist monks have found a new popularity with today's health-conscious citizens.

CONFUCIANISM

The Buddhist culture flourished into the Koryo dynasty (935–1392). However, although the monks still wielded some influence, the kings of the Koryo dynasty adopted a Chinese governmental approach, which brought the influence of Confucianism to the country and moved the country away from vegetarianism.

Towards the end of the Koryo dynasty the Mongols took control of Korea and ruled for around 100 years, before being ousted by General Yi Seong-Gye, who seized political and military power and, in 1392, established the amazingly long-lived Chosun (Yi)

Above: A group of novice Buddhist monks in Seoul, aged between 5 and 7, sheltering from the rain after a head-shaving ceremony to celebrate Buddha's birthday.

Above: A Confucian temple in South Korea. Based on the teachings of a Chinese sage, Confucianism is based around the importance of morality, and the cultivation of the civilized individual. The philosophy has had a significant influence on Korea.

dynasty, which ruled for over 500 years until 1910. Confucianism became the state creed, and the Chinese influence steadily took hold, heralding a new era in the national cuisine.

CHINESE INGREDIENTS

Closer ties with China meant that a wide range of spices and seasonings became available, an important driving influence in determining flavour trends. Black pepper and vinegar, molasses and rice wine were now enjoyed by many Koreans.

Tofu was another Chinese ingredient that had a tremendous impact when introduced to Korea. Its ubiquity in Korean cooking, and versatility in different dishes, has meant it is now more popular in Korea than in its native China. Many other dishes from China were introduced after the Korean War, with Chinese restaurants becoming very popular. However, over the past five decades their recipes have been adapted to create popular dishes that are distinctly Korean in their use of local ingredients and spices.

JAPANESE RULE

The Japanese asserted their authority over their neighbours in the 19th and 20th centuries, attempting to impose by the use of force their own religion and education system, and even the adoption of Japanese names by the Koreans. The Koreans fought back with their own independence movement, and after the Second World War, gained freedom from the Japanese.

However, the period of Japanese colonial rule brought many different ingredients to Korea, including the *inari maki* roll and *udon* noodles. While the preparation and cooking methods have remained the same as in Japan, the choice of sauces and spices gives a uniquely Korean taste to these dishes, and these adaptations have travelled back to Japan where they are becoming increasingly popular.

THE SEPARATION OF NORTH AND SOUTH

Since the division of Korea into North and South in 1953, after the Korean War, the country has been physically divided by a DMZ (De-Militarized Zone) roughly along the 38th parallel, and the North has withdrawn into isolation from the rest of the world, while the South has enthusiastically embraced the technology and industry of the 21st-century world.

The harmony of opposites

One of the fundamental principles of Eastern philosophy is that of the two universal opposing forces of yin and yang. This concept has a strong influence on Koreans' thinking and their approach to cooking, and is reflected in the ingredients selected by chefs when preparing dishes with the intention of achieving harmony in flavour, colour and presentation. Traditional Korean cooking – from the dishes of the royal court to simple family meals – uses green, red, yellow, white and black ingredients in equal amounts, to ensure evenness in the diet and to reflect the theory of the five elements from traditional Chinese philosophy: wood, fire, earth, metal and water. The dishes will also have harmonizing yin and yang values: hot and spicy yang foods stimulate the body, whereas cool yin foods calm and nourish the system. Neutral foods are a balance of yin and yang. The perfect meal will contain yang dishes to heat up the body and yin dishes to cool down the brain.

Above: The ceremonial dress of the Confucianist village of Chunghak-dong.

VEGETARIAN CUISINE

Although the cuisine of Korea does feature meat and fish quite heavily, there is a strong vegetarian tradition largely due to the influences of Buddhism. Despite the cross-cultural exchanges with China and Japan, and the significant influence they have both had on the evolution of Korean cuisine, it remains quite distinct from either. The cuisines of all the countries share the same balance of salty, bitter, hot, sweet and sour – the "five flavours" – but cooking techniques and ingredients create a marked culinary difference between the three.

THE SPECIALITIES OF KOREA

In Korea, certain key flavours such as garlic, ginger and soy sauce lend themselves to common preparation techniques such as pickling or grilling (broiling). Then there are the signature dishes, such as *kimchi* (pickled vegetables, often cabbage), *sangchae* (tangy, crunchy salads) and *namul* (vegetable side dishes).

One might expect the Koreans to stir-fry in a wok like the Chinese, or eat ingredients raw like the Japanese, as these characteristics would be consistent with their geographical proximity. However, the Koreans have developed their own methods of

cooking, including preservation techniques that give their cuisine a unique array of flavours.

From mild rice dishes and delicate soups, through to pickled vegetables and fiery noodle salads, there is something wonderfully mysterious about the taste of Korean food. Whereas the flavours in Chinese and Thai dishes are easily identifiable, Korean cooking blends fresh and preserved ingredients to create complex tastes. In Korea there is also a

Above: The method of making kimchi *varies greatly from region to region, but it always contains fermented vegetables*

generosity of spirit and a desire to share and please, which characterize the experience of eating.

CHARACTERISTIC FLAVOURS

As in Japan, rice, noodles, pickles and fresh vegetables form the basis of a vegetarian diet. However, the spices and marinades are distinctive to Korea.

Above: Short grain rice, a favourite in Korea, has a distinctive stickiness.

Above: The heat of chillies has become intrinsic to Korean cooking, but their fire is just one element of this multi-layered cuisine which balances several flavours.

Food is predominantly seasoned with
the traditional key flavours of garlic,
ginger, soy sauce, spring onions
(scallions) and sesame oil, plus the
careful use of sugar and rice vinegar.
The Koreans are the greatest consumers
of garlic in the whole of Asia. Delicious
spice pastes are used in many dishes
with either the fermented soya bean
paste, *doenjang*, or the ubiquitous
gochujang, red chilli paste, providing
the foundation of a multitude of recipes.

Koreans tend to make a
combination of freshly prepared and
preserved foods for each meal, rather
than preparing just one main dish.
The strong taste of Korean food
originates both from their love of
pungent flavours, and from the
preservation techniques that allow
those flavours to develop and intensify.

In addition Koreans make use of
ingredients in different ways to their
neighbours; for example, sesame seeds
are always toasted before being added
to cooking, to emphasize their nutty
flavour. By enhancing certain flavours,
and mixing fresh and pickled tastes,
Korea has found a culinary identity
unlike any other in Asia.

With globalization and the influence
of the Western food industry, Korean
cuisine is evolving at a dramatic rate.
However, despite these multicultural
influences, the basic diet remains the
same as it has for centuries.

THE INTRODUCTION OF RICE

Rice proved itself early in the country's
history as a staple ingredient for the
Korean diet. It grows well in the varying
climate, and its inviting taste and the

ease with which it could be cooked also
had a great effect on the cuisine. Rice
became an essential feature of most
meals, adopting the same role as bread
in the West, and played a major part in
establishing the Korean style of eating.
It was served as the foundation of the
meal, and around this began to grow
the idea of cooking a number of small
accompanying dishes of soup, salads,
and vegetables. Having rice at every
meal, and in many dishes, also helped
to form the Koreans' sociable way of
eating, with each diner partaking freely
of any dish on the table.

THE CHILLI PEPPER

Another revolutionary event in Korean
culinary history was the introduction of
the chilli pepper in the 16th century.
In 1592 and 1597 the Japanese
invaded Korea, but they were eventually
beaten off in 1598 with help from the
Chinese. Catholic priests from Portugal
travelled with the Japanese troops and

*Above: After rice, garlic is the second-
largest cash crop in Korea, most of
which is grown in the south-west.*

brought with them the chilli plants and
seeds from the New World – a long
round trip from South America to Asia,
via Europe. Prior to this, spiciness had
been imparted with the Chinese
Sichuan peppercorn, but Korean cooks
were wholeheartedly seduced by the
flavour and heat of the chilli pepper.

The Koreans adored spicy food, and
created *gochujang*, a red chilli paste
that has become a basic ingredient in
every Korean kitchen. Countless dishes
were built upon its fiery kick, and
traditional techniques for preserving
vegetables were brought to life with
its strong, pungent flavour. Koreans
believe that red is a colour which
offers protection from the devil, and
this may also have had a bearing on
the all-pervading use of *gochujang*
in their cooking.

Eating & Drinking Traditions

Left: Villagers enjoy a traditional Korean meal which is accompanied by soju, *a distilled grain liquor.*

All Korean meals are designed to include a harmonious assortment of dishes, and to enjoy the experience of Korean dining fully this is the perfect approach. When you are preparing any of the recipes in this book you should choose a number of dishes – maybe three or four – of contrasting texture and colour, and varying in taste, and serve them together with a dish of rice and a bowl of soup for each person. You will then be sampling a Korean evening meal as it would be eaten in many family homes throughout the peninsula, from a farmhouse in the chilly northern mountains to a high-rise apartment in the bustling cities of the south.

A VARIETY OF TASTES

A typical vegetarian Korean meal will have a selection of small dishes, rather than a single main dish for each person, and all the food is served together rather than as different courses. A main vegetable dish is traditionally accompanied by rice, soup and salad, along with a selection of pickled vegetables, or *kimchi*. The dishes will reflect a range of preparation techniques as well as different ingredients – maybe steamed rice, a simmered casserole of vegetables, braised or fried tofu and boiled dumplings.

The main dishes are shared between all the diners. Because of this style of eating there is a real spirit of fellowship when dining Korean-style, and this is accentuated by the common practice of cooking food on a gas or charcoal grill at the table, giving mealtimes an inviting, domestic feel.

While the idea of sharing an abundance of small dishes is the same as the Spanish *tapas* style of dining, the Korean approach requires all the dishes to complement each other. To this end, the recipes of certain dishes will be altered depending on the other dishes being served so that all the elements work in harmony with each other.

Traditional Korean dining
Although there is no prescribed order for eating the many dishes served at a traditional meal, many Koreans like to start with a small taste of soup before then sharing the other dishes among themselves. The formation of menus will vary depending on the number of dishes and the occasion, from a mere three or four for an informal family supper to many exotic and glamorous dishes at major celebrations for weddings, special birthdays and festivals.

Right: Koreans taking tea in a tea house. A low table and floor seating is the traditional practice.

TABLE SETTINGS

The classic Korean table setting is one of the most impressive aspects of Korean cuisine and is quite unique, both in its selection of dishes and in its form of presentation. As in other Asian countries, an individual bowl of soup and a dish of rice are provided for every person dining. However, what sets the Korean table distinctively apart from its Asian neighbours is the fact that all the dishes are served simultaneously rather than as one course after another.

The most common table setting is based around the serving of a bowl of rice as the main dish, known in Korean as *bansang* or *bapsang*. Directly translated, *ban* or *bap* means cooked rice and *sang* means table, and this form holds true for other table settings. On a traditional *bansang* table setting the main rice dish would be served with soup, a plate of *kimchi* and a selection of side dishes referred to as *chups*.

Below: A traditional Korean tea ceremony in Seoul, South Korea, forming part of a wedding celebration.

TEA DRINKING

Koreans tend to drink mainly water or *boricha*, a tea brewed from roasted barley, with their meals. Green tea is also very popular; this is a drink that was introduced with the rise of Buddhism in the 7th century as an indispensable part of temple ceremonies. During the Koryo dynasty (918–1392) tea became popular among the upper classes and nobility, too, even finding a place in the rituals of the royal court.

ALCOHOL

Koreans also drink a wide range of alcoholic beverages including the local wine, *chungju*, a variety of domestically brewed beers, and *makgoli*, a potent milky-white rice drink. However, the most famous drink in Korea is *soju*, a rough rice wine with a fearsome kick, which was traditionally distilled in Buddhist monasteries. The popularity of *soju* cannot be overestimated, and no Korean meal is really complete without a glass of this potent liquor.

Koreans will never pour their own drinks; they believe it is courteous for their companion to pour it for them. Accepting the drink is more important than actually drinking it; declining the first glass is considered terribly impolite,

and it is better to accept the glass and simply touch it against the lips than to refuse it entirely.

The correct amount to drink is a matter of some debate in Korea. Traditional wisdom is summed up by an old saying, which translates as "Don't stop after one glass; three glasses is lacking, five glasses is proper and seven glasses is excessive."

VEGETABLES, SALADS & TOFU

The Korean diet is generally a healthy one. The food is mainly low in fat and high in nutrients, with an emphasis on fresh, seasonal food cooked at home and served to be eaten immediately. When fresh ingredients are not available, there is the spicy concoction *kimchi*, which preserves both nutrients and flavour by excluding light and heat in a sealed jar.

Vegetables and salads are a vital part of the Korean diet. They balance the solid base of rice and its accompanying protein, and provide essential vitamins and minerals, and a crucial contrast in flavour, colour and texture.

Vegetables can form the basis of a soup or stew, or be eaten as a main dish in their own right. They make up the majority of the side dishes which are set out for diners to share, featuring any number of vegetables such as aubergine (eggplant), radish, sweet potatoes and mushrooms. There may also be a basket of lettuce or chrysanthemum leaves on the table as an accompaniment. Lastly, of course,

there will be a dish or two of *kimchi*, maybe based on cabbage, radish or turnip.

The high consumption of tofu is linked to Korea's Buddhist roots and to its relatively limited meat resources. Made from sweet soya beans, tofu is still Korea's main source of protein.

KOREAN VEGETABLES

Vegetable and salad dishes vary according to the season. Staples are:

Chinese cabbage

Called *baechu* or *tong baechu* in Korea, this is also commonly known as napa cabbage or Chinese leaves, and nowadays can be found in most supermarkets. It has a long white leaf, and looks quite unlike other round cabbage varieties. It is the key ingredient for traditional *kimchi*.

Chinese white radish

This giant of the radish family can grow to an impressive 30cm/1ft long, and is thick, similar in character to a large parsnip.

Also known by its Japanese name of *daikon* or its Hindi name of *mooli*, this vegetable is simply known in Korea as *moo*. It has an inherent spiciness and sweetness and a pungent flavour.

Perilla

Commonly known as wild sesame leaf, perilla is also called *kenip*. These wonderfully fragrant leaves are used in many ways in the kitchen, and while they look similar to Japanese *shiso*, the flavour is slightly different. The refreshing properties of this herb bring out a naturally fresh taste in many dishes.

Korean chives

These are similar to Chinese chives in terms of flavour and texture and in Korea are called *buchu*. Korean chives are flat green vegetables and are larger than the herb variety more familiar in Western cooking. This delicate vegetable bruises easily so it should be handled and washed with great care.

Above: Cabbage is most commonly found in kimchi, *widely expounded as one of the world's healthiest foods.*

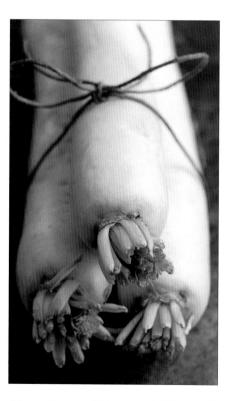

Above: Peppery Chinese radish is usually served cooked, unlike the smaller radishes common to Western kitchens.

Above: Korean food is an amalgamation of carefully constructed flavours; pungent garlic is one of the most popular.

Above: Perilla leaves are reminiscent of mint and delicious in salads.

Right: Soft, sweet mung beans are a Korean staple.

Mung beans

These small round green beans can be used in mung bean soufflé and several other recipes. The sprouts of the mung bean are also a valuable ingredient, used to make soup and often added to stir-fries. Mung beansprouts are favoured over other beansprouts as they have an intense nutty flavour and a pleasing crunchy texture.

Leeks

Koreans use *daepa*, a large variety of the spring onion (scallion) that is sweeter and more flavourful than the small green onion. However, leeks have a similar flavour, and the two are interchangeable.

Spring onions (scallions)

These are the most popular garnish for soups and other dishes, sometimes shredded into elaborate shapes like little brushes. Spring onions crop up everywhere, including in *kimchi* recipes, stir-fries, soups, stews and flavoured rice. The Korean variant is virtually identical to the Western equivalent.

Garlic

This staple ingredient is added to many dishes, and features as a pickled vegetable in its own right, ready to use during the winter when fresh garlic is not available. It comes into its own in the *kimchi* pot, where its full flavour complements the spices, salt and spring onions (scallions).

Minari

This is a small salad leaf with a wonderful aroma, similar in appearance to watercress, and with a long, crunchy stem. It is used in stews and salads, or can be simply blanched and served with a sweet and sour chilli paste dressing. Watercress can be successfully substituted.

Chrysanthemum leaves

Known as *sukgot* in Korea and cooked in a similar way to spinach, these leaves are strongly aromatic and are often used to suppress the smell of strong flavours in certain dishes. This herb, with its wonderfully exotic fragrance, can only be found in Korean stores, but the flat-leaf Italian parsley makes a good substitute.

Fern fronds

Also known as "fiddlehead ferns", fern fronds are rarely used in the Western kitchen. Wild ferns can be poisonous, so use the dried fern fronds, available at any Asian store. Used as a key ingredient in *yukgejang* soup, these are also seasoned and sautéed for salads.

Above: Korean chives are delicately flavoured and make an attractive and tasty garnish.

Above: Beautifully nutty and full of protein, mung beansprouts are a tasty and nutritious ingredient.

Above: Sweet potatoes are used in sweet and savoury dishes.

Above: Dried kelp imbues soups and stocks with a salty sweetness.

Above: Rice rolls, wrapped in nori, make a delicious lunchtime treat.

Sweet potatoes

This pink or orange-fleshed root vegetable was brought to Korea by the Japanese and quickly became established as a staple food. Sweet potatoes are eaten in both savoury dishes such as stir-fries, where their subtle flavour blends beautifully with mushrooms and garlic, as well as in sweet dishes such as Sweet Potato Jelly (see page 92), where they are cooked until soft.

Mushrooms

There are several varieties which lend their strong, distinctive flavours to many Korean dishes.

- *Shiitake mushrooms* Called *pyogo* in Korean, these have a flat round cap, and are dark brown with an earthy flavour. Bought fresh or dried, if dried, they should be soaked in warm water to reconstitute.
- *Enoki mushrooms* Also known as *enokitake* in Japanese, enoki mushrooms have a long, thin stem and tiny cap and an extremely delicate, slightly furry texture. They are generally used for garnishing.
- *Oyster mushrooms* A delicate pale grey colour and fan-shaped, oyster mushrooms are often used for casseroles and stir-fried dishes, being mild in taste and silky in texture.

SEAWEED

Used in Korean cooking for centuries, seaweed has a high vitamin and protein content. Three kinds of seaweed are:

Dried kelp

This seaweed is known as *dashikonbu* in Japanese or *dahima* in Korean, and can be found in Asian stores. It has a rich sea flavour, perfectly suited to making soup stock and salads. Kelp should always be soaked before being used.

Nori

This is the Japanese term for the popular edible flat layer of seaweed known as *kim* in Korea. It has a colour somewhere between dark blue and black, and is sold dried in small, very thin sheets. It has a crisp texture and a salty flavour with a distinctly toasty aroma, and is used to make the rice rolls so popular as snacks and lunchbox items in Korea.

Above: Shiitake mushrooms, dried and reconstituted with water, are considered to have superior flavour to fresh.

Above: Fresh enoki mushrooms are mild and fruity, with a delicate crunchy texture that is enjoyed cooked and raw.

Above: Oyster mushrooms are firm and tasty and are an ideal way to add flavour and substance to light meals.

Miyuk

An edible seaweed, known as *wakame* in Japan, *miyuk* is much softer than dried kelp, and contains a range of vitamins that promote good circulation. A popular Korean soup, which is traditionally served at birthday celebrations, is made from *miyuk*. This is also given to new mothers as it is believed to improve the circulation and to help them to regain their strength after childbirth.

Above: Nutritious tofu is the perfect meat substitute.

TOFU

This beancurd cake is made from the milky liquid extracted from soya beans, in a method similar to cheesemaking, with sweet soya beans replacing the milk. Tofu is a good vegetarian option that is commonly used as a meat substitute, and has been a principal source of protein for Koreans since the 15th century, and is often combined with vegetables. It is both delicious and easy to cook, and you'll rarely find a Korean meal that does not include tofu. Traditional tofu dishes include fried tofu, tofu soup (with vegetables and noodles), tofu cooked in soy sauce, and *tofu chige* (a spicy soup).

Firm tofu, which is widely available at supermarkets, is pressed from fresh tofu to remove some of the water. It has a much longer product life, but it is not considered as special as fresh tofu.

GRILL ACCOMPANIMENTS – *NAMUL*

Dishes that are grilled are frequently accompanied by side orders of fresh mushrooms, garlic, potatoes and other vegetables in Korea. These side dishes are known as *namul*.

Namul recipes vary considerably. Any type of any available vegetable may be used, and any part of the plant. What is more, these little dishes of radish, cucumber, potato, mushroom, and so on can be served separately or mixed in tasteful combinations to make a powerful range of colours, textures and tastes in one dish.

Namul vegetables are often steamed or stir-fried quickly in order to preserve their vitamins. They can also be served raw and crunchy, or preserved, fermented, as *kimchi*.

Right: This namul *combines soya beansprouts, leeks and sesame oil with a garnish of red chilli.*

Shredded spring onion (scallion)

The ubiquitous spring onion (scallion) often appears as an addition to the lettuce leaf wrap – just a pinch of shredded spring onions will give an enhanced zesty flavour. Here is the recipe for this tasty garnish. Serve with tofu or vegetable dishes that are in need of an extra zing.

SERVES 4

INGREDIENTS
1/2 leek or 4 spring onions
  (scallions)
30ml/2 tbsp *gochujang*
  (Korean chilli powder)
30ml/2 tbsp sugar
30ml/2 tbsp cider vinegar
10ml/2 tsp sesame oil
cold water

2 Combine the *gochujang*, sugar, vinegar and sesame oil in a small bowl, and mix thoroughly.

1 Thinly shred the spring onions, discarding the bulb, and leave to soak in cold water for 5 minutes to make them crunchy.

3 Add the spring onions and coat with the chilli mixture before serving.

KIMCHI & FERMENTED FOODS

Koreans have developed various ways of preserving food. In the days before refrigeration this enabled them to eat well during the winter when fresh vegetables and salads, fresh meat or seafood were unavailable. The tangy, spicy taste of these foods is now associated with Korean cuisine.

Kimchi

Consisting of pickled vegetables and other foodstuffs preserved in earthenware pots, *kimchi* is Korea's most famous culinary export. Made for over 2,000 years, it is believed to be a life-giving dish which encourages good health and stamina. Although any pickled and fermented vegetable mixture can be called *kimchi*, the best-known variety is made with napa cabbage. The vegetables are coated with a mixture that typically includes chilli, ginger, garlic and soy sauce, and then sealed in a jar and left to ferment until the flavours have blended. Koreans pickle most vegetables like this, including radishes, cucumber, turnip and aubergine (eggplant), as well as occasionally fruit. During the fermentation process the vegetables lose much of their flavour, adopting the tastes of the seasonings, but with a greatly enhanced texture.

Kimchi is most often eaten as a side dish at any meal, breakfast, lunch or dinner. However, it also makes a tasty accompaniment to little fried street snacks made of rice and sesame seeds, or may be covered with a thin batter and fried as *kimchi* fritters (*buchimgae*).

Kimchi can also be used in a spicy stew with vegetables such as mushrooms and onions, and tofu for protein. This is simmered on the stove until everything is really hot and all the textures are soft. Koreans would eat the stew with a crunchy vegetable and some glutinous rice for balance.

There are many *kimchi* variations from the different provinces according to which vegetables are available. For instance, from the province of *Gyeonggi* comes a recipe for turnip *kimchi* made with light soy sauce, chilli and garlic, onions and salt.

Although *kimchi* is generally made only from vegetables, some varieties that can be found in Asian stores or restaurants can contain fish or seafood, or are made using fish or anchovy sauce. It is important to always check before you buy or order *kimchi* that it is in fact vegetarian.

Other fermented foods

Doenjang (soya bean paste) is also fermented and can be preserved for months, taken from the store cupboard whenever needed to brighten a winter stew or vegetable soup.

Left: Traditional cabbage kimchi *– the most famous of Korean dishes. The making of* kimchi *is considered an art. Below:* Doenjang, *fermented soy bean, is a Korean store-cupboard essential.*

A basic *kimchi* recipe

INGREDIENTS
1 *napa* cabbage (Chinese leaf)
15ml/1 tsp salt, plus salt for brine
15ml/1 tsp sugar
15ml/1 tsp chilli pepper flakes
15ml/1 tsp pine nuts
15ml/1 tsp fresh ginger
15ml/1 tsp fresh garlic
15ml/1 tsp light soy sauce
a handful of watercress
a handful of green onions
a handful of sliced radish

1 Cut the *napa* cabbage into two.

2 Submerge the cabbage in a couple of handfuls of sea salt and water to cover. Soak for 6 hours, then rinse.

3 Combine the remaining ingredients to form the seasoning.

4 Cut out and discard the hard core of the cabbage halves, and pack the seasoning between each leaf. Wrap one outer leaf tightly around the remaining leaves, and put it all into a sealed ceramic container. Leave for 40 hours and then refrigerate.

RICE & NOODLES

The rich spiciness of many Korean dishes needs a plain, starchy foil, and this contrast is provided by rice and noodles.

RICE

The foundation of all Korean meals, rice dishes are eaten throughout the day. In combination with soup and vegetables it forms an essential part of a nutritious and satisfying Korean meal. Koreans believe that their strength comes from the continuing consumption of rice.

Rice is traditionally cooked on its own in the Korean kitchen, although sometimes other grains such as millet and barley are included to enhance the flavour. Beans and chestnuts are occasionally included with rice dishes, and cooked vegetables are often mixed into the dish before serving. The Koreans, just like the Japanese, eat only the sticky short and medium grain varieties.

Short grain rice

This is the staple food of Korea. Called *ssal* in Korean, this is close in shape and texture to Japanese rice. It becomes soft and sticky when cooked.

Brown rice

This is normally cooked as a mixture with white rice and other grains, and is considered to have better nutritional value than the common short grain rice.

Glutinous or sweet rice

Slightly longer than the common short grain rice, this is only used in rice cakes, cookies and other sweet dishes, where the grains need to bind together.

Mixed grains

Rice grain mixtures are popular in Korea. They vary from region to region, but typically contain combinations of brown rice, sweet rice, wild rice, barley, hulled millet, green peas, yellow peas, black-eyed beans (peas), kidney beans and red beans. The Korean dish called Five-grain rice, or *Ogokbap* combines four other grains (including millet, black beans and sweet beans) with regular rice. Other ingredients can be added, such as soya beansprouts and chestnuts.

Right: Pudding or sweet rice is short and fat with a white kernel. When cooked, it becomes glutinous. It is useful as a binder for gravies, sauces, and fillings, or in sweet dishes.

NOODLES

Korean noodles can be made of different grains and vegetables, the most common being wheat, buckwheat and sweet potato. They are almost as common as rice in Korean cuisine. Noodles should be boiled for a few minutes in lots of water but should never be over-cooked, especially for a stir-fried dish.

Glass noodles

Known as *dangmyun*, these delicate strands of sweet potato starch are also known as cellophane noodles, Chinese vermicelli, bean threads and bean thread noodles. They are often used as the base for noodle soups or stir-fried dishes, and can also be added to casseroles to provide volume and richness of flavour and texture.

Above: Originally from Japan, udon noodles are thicker and softer than other types of noodle.

Buckwheat and wheat noodles

Thin and brown in colour, buckwheat noodles are known in Korea as *memil*. They have a distinctive crunchy texture and are similar in appearance to a softer variety called *momil*, which are made from wheat flour. These are much better known as the Japanese *soba* noodle.

Udon noodles

Handmade flat noodles, also called udon noodles or *kalguksu*, are made from plain wheat flour and are popular for dishes where a more tender texture is suitable.

Somyun

A thin, white noodle made from plain flour, which is often used for noodles served in broth.

Soba noodles

These noodles, of Japanese origin, are made of buckwheat flour (*soba-ko*) and wheat flour (*komugi-ko*). They are of approximately the same thickness as spaghetti, and are prepared in various hot and cold dishes in Korea. They can be bought dried, but they taste best when freshly handmade.

TRADITIONAL FLAVOURINGS

Seasoning food carefully and plentifully is a must in Korea. Not only was this habitual because spices would preserve food for the months of scarcity during the cold winters, but Korean cooks make sure that the tastes of individual spices blend with each other and the base of vegetables or tofu. Furthermore, the influence of Buddhism can be felt in the belief that balanced seasoning leads to good health – the yin and yang of salty and sweet, spicy and mild makes for a general equilibrium in the body.

The traditional technique of seasoning, known in Korea as *yangnyum*, requires a mixture of spices to be blended with almost medicinal precision. Koreans believe there are five elements – fire, earth, water, wood and metal – that govern everyone's life, and these have their direct counterparts in cooking flavours. The five flavours, salty, sweet, sour, spicy and bitter, balance each other and so should be combined as far as possible at each meal.

The basic seasonings used to create the five different flavours include salt, soy sauce, *gochujang* chilli paste, *doenjang* soya bean paste, vinegar and sugar. Aromatic seasonings include ginger, mustard, pepper, sesame oil, sesame seeds, spring onions (scallions), garlic and

Above: Soy sauce is a regular component of Korean meals.

chrysanthemum leaves. Most Korean dishes are cooked with at least half a dozen different ingredients and seasonings, producing a complex and distinctive taste.

THE THREE MAJOR FLAVOURINGS

While any self-respecting Korean cook would insist on using many different ingredients, there are three flavourings that dominate Korean cuisine and without which almost no Korean recipe is complete. These are:

- soy sauce
- soya bean paste, *doenjang*
- red chilli paste, *gochujang*

The actual process of making *doenjang*, *gochujang* and soy sauce from scratch is a lengthy and complex one. Nowadays few households still make these condiments, relying instead on store-bought alternatives as basic ingredients, which they then combine in traditional and time-honoured recipes for strong marinades, sauces and dips.

Soy sauce

There are a number of types of soy sauce, the by-product of *doenjang* paste. Light soy sauce is used in soups and to season vegetables, while dark soy sauce is used for roasted, steamed and more hearty dishes.

Soy dip

This dip is widely served with Korean fritters and dumplings, as well as tofu and tempura dishes.

SERVES 4

INGREDIENTS
45ml/3 tbsp dark soy sauce
1 garlic clove, chopped
15ml/1 tbsp cider vinegar
7.5ml/1½ tsp sesame oil
5ml/1 tsp ground sesame seeds

Mix all the ingredients together thoroughly and transfer to a small sauce bowl for dipping.

Doenjang

This paste is made of fermented soya beans. The beans are cooked and dried into blocks, then once the fermentation process has begun with a fine mould appearing on the surface of the blocks, they are added to water and kept in a

Above: Chrysanthemum leaves are used in food, to make tea and as an ingredient in Korean rice wine.

Above: Doenjang *paste, made from fermented soya beans, is commonly used to augment soups and stews.*

Above: Gochujang *is a distinctive dark red chilli paste, its extensive use demonstrates the Korean love of chillies!*

warm place to continue fermenting. Once the process is complete, the liquid is drained off to make soy sauce, and the solids are made into *doenjang*, a salty, tasty paste similar to Japanese miso, ideal for adding a sparkle to stews and soups or for spreading on vegetables such as sticks of celery.

Gochujang

The classic Korean paste called *gochujang* also uses soya beans as a base, but this time red chillies are added for spice, as well as powdered rice, salt and a little honey or sugar, before the mixture is left to ferment in a warm place. This produces a dark red, rich, concentrated paste which is used to cover tofu or vegetables and is added to many cooked dishes to give them a spicy tang.

Above: This sauce combines gochujang *and* doenjang *to make a versatile paste.*

Chilli paste and vinegar sauce

This versatile uncooked sauce, called *cho gochujang*, is known for its tart piquancy and can be used as either a dip or a dressing with any salad, rice or noodle dish.

SERVES 4

INGREDIENTS
60ml/4 tbsp *gochujang*
  chilli paste
75ml/5 tbsp water
60ml/4 tbsp cider vinegar
15ml/1 tbsp lemon juice
30ml/2 tbsp sugar
2 garlic cloves, crushed
30ml/2 tbsp spring onions
  (scallions), finely chopped
5ml/1 tsp sesame seeds
15ml/1 tbsp sesame oil

1 Combine all the ingredients in a bowl and mix them together.

2 Transfer the final chilli and vinegar paste to a small sauce bowl before serving it to accompany any Korean salad dish, or with Chinese leaves.

Stir-fried *gochujang* chilli paste

This sauce, called *yangnyum gochujang*, is often used for the traditional rice dish *bibimbap*.

SERVES 4

INGREDIENTS
15ml/1 tbsp sesame oil
65g/2¹/₂oz Quorn mince
2 garlic cloves, crushed
250ml/8fl oz/1 cup *gochujang*
  chilli paste
30ml/2 tbsp maple syrup
15ml/1 tbsp sugar

2 Add the chilli paste and 45ml/ 3 tbsp of water, and stir until it has formed a sticky paste.

3 Add the maple syrup and the sugar, and simmer the mixture in the pan for a further 30 seconds before then transferring to a sauce bowl to serve.

1 Coat a wok or pan with sesame oil and heat over medium heat. Add the Quorn mince and garlic, and stir-fry until lightly golden brown.

SPICES, HERBS & SEEDS

SPICES

The aromas of *doenjang* (soya bean paste), *gochujang* (chilli) paste and soy sauce pervade the Korean kitchen. However, there are many other favourite flavourings. No Korean cook would consider serving a meal that was predominantly flavoured with only one spice; a mixture should be used to make sure that the balance and harmony of the food is just right.

Garlic

This essential aromatic vegetable is used for everything from seasoning soup to creating marinades. It is also used whole as an accompaniment for grilled dishes.

Above: Garlic's pungent flavour makes it a frequent ingredient in Korean cooking.

Chilli

The chilli pepper is the next most important flavouring after garlic. The Korean version varies from mild to fiery, and, combined with garlic, forms the basis of *kimchi* flavouring.

Above: Chillies only came to Korea in the 16th century, but their fiery heat quickly made them a popular ingredient.

Dried chilli

A single sun-dried red chilli can be used to create a sharp, spicy taste, or used flaked or whole for garnishing and presentation. Sun-dried chillies are often ground into chilli powder, milder than the Indian version, which forms the basis of many Korean recipes.

Ginger

The distinctive sweet piquant taste of ginger is popular all over Asia. Korean cooks, as well as using it in *kimchi*, like to combine its taste with that of other ingredients, creating a new subtle flavour.

Above: The warmth of ginger adds depth to any dish.

Ginseng

A root best known for its medicinal properties and widely used in Korea to make tea, ginseng is also used in cooking, particularly in the summer chicken soup *samgyetang*.

Maca

This green herbal root originates in Peru, and is believed to have strong medicinal and energy-giving qualities.

Right: The green powder of the maca root.

Mustard

A favourite accompaniment, the pungency of mustard sauce combines well with saltier dishes. It is made by mixing dried mustard powder with vinegar, water and a little sugar and salt.

Sesame leaves

These leaves are traditionally used as a green vegetable and have a strong nutty aroma. They are also used in salads and as wraps to eat with rice and *miso*.

Above: Sesame leaves, as well as sesame oil and sesame seeds, are used as flavourings.

HERBS

Green herbs are not generally added to Korean food, and are more likely to be made into tea. Various mixtures of herbs and spices to aid digestion and promote good health have traditionally been concocted to drink after a meal, but the commonest are those made with ginseng, roasted barley or ginger.

NUTS AND SEEDS

Sesame seeds

These are toasted to bring out the distinctive taste, and used as both flavouring and garnish in many recipes. They are also toasted and crushed for sweet or savoury snacks.

Gingko nuts

Used in sweet and savoury dishes, gingko nuts are also served as an alternative to lotus seeds. Grilled and salted, they are a popular snack in both Japan and Korea, and once cooked they turn a delicate shade of green.

Above: The versatility of gingko nuts means that they are used in both sweet and savoury dishes.

STOCK

A good, tasty stock is an essential base for many of the Korean recipes that are introduced here. They will give the depth of flavour that is essential to give an authentic Korean taste to the dish.

A small bowl of soup, steamed rice and some tasty vegetable salads and *namul* (side dishes) are the backbone of a typical vegetarian Korean meal. Soup is not served as a separate course, but it is often the first thing a Korean diner will taste while stews are boiling or stirfries are being prepared, keeping hunger pangs at bay with its savoury flavours. At dinner time, soup is usually served in a small dish, one for each person, placed next to the individual rice dish.

One of the most delightful ways to taste this flavoursome brew is while strolling around the town and socializing with friends – it is a common sight to see little cups of piquant soup for sale next to the rice dishes, pancakes and fritters on the stalls of street vendors.

Koreans cook soup, using all sorts of ingredients from meat and vegetables to tofu and seaweed. What they all have in common is a strong, often home-made stock base and a fiery kick from added chillies, garlic and spices. Korean soup, packed with ingredients, tends to be a heartier dish than many other Asian

Above: A steaming bowl of hot and spicy potato and courgette soup, a delicious and aromatic medley of tastes.

Asian vegetable stock

This is a well-known and versatile vegetable stock that can be used for Korean dishes. It is great as a base for soups and for fortifying the taste of hearty stews or casserole dishes.

MAKES 1 LITRE/1³/₄ PINTS/4 CUPS

INGREDIENTS
2 stalks of lemon grass
10g/¹/₄oz fresh root ginger
150g/6oz spring onions (scallions)
2 carrots
90g/3¹/₂oz Chinese white radish
1 leek
1 stalk of celery
4 large mushrooms
3 garlic cloves, peeled
1 tbsp tamarind paste
2¹/₂ tbsp/35ml soy sauce
salt and ground black pepper
2 litres/3 pints/8¹/₂ cups water

1 Chop the lemon grass, ginger, spring onions (scallions), carrots, radish, leek and celery into medium chunks. Slice the mushrooms.

2 Put all the chopped and sliced vegetables into a large pot with the garlic cloves, tamarind paste, soy sauce, salt and pepper.

3 Pour the 2 litres/3 pints/8¹/₂ cups of water into the pan over the vegetables and bring to a gentle boil over a medium heat.

4 Skim off the foam that rises to the surface, frequently at first and then from time to time.

5 Turn up the heat and cook over a high heat until the liquid has reduced by half. Top up the pan with an equivalent amount of water and allow the liquid to reduce again. Repeat one more time until you have just over 1 litre/1³/₄ pints/4 cups of stock left in the pan.

6 Strain the stock, discarding the solids then pour into a sealable container.

7 Refrigerate or freeze for future use in soups and casseroles.

KIMCHI &
QUICK BITES

Quick bites are an integral part of the Korean

national cuisine, and there are over a hundred types of kimchi,

made from vegetables seasoned with garlic and chilli.

Rich in vitamins and minerals, kimchi boast a unique flavour.

Alternative snacks include light and crunchy Vegetable Fritters,

which make a tasty treat, tempting traditional dishes like Steamed

Tofu and Chive Dumplings, or for after a meal,

Sweet Cinnamon Pancakes.

CABBAGE KIMCHI

MADE WITH CHINESE LEAVES, THIS IS THE CLASSIC VARIETY OF KIMCHI AND THE ONE MOST LIKELY TO BE FOUND AT ANY MEAL. THE SPICINESS OF THE CHILLI CONTRASTS WITH THE LIGHT SOY SAUCE AND A HINT OF TANGY SPRING ONION. THIS DISH TAKES A MINIMUM OF TWO DAYS TO PREPARE.

SERVES TEN

INGREDIENTS

1 head Chinese leaves (Chinese cabbage), about 2kg/4¹/₂lb
salt

For the marinade

50g/2oz/¹/₄ cup coarse sea salt
75ml/5 tbsp water
30ml/2 tbsp table salt

For the seasoning

¹/₂ Chinese white radish, about 500g/1¹/₄lb
25g/1oz Korean chives
25g/1oz *minari*, watercress or rocket (arugula)
5 garlic cloves
15g/¹/₂oz fresh root ginger, peeled
¹/₂ onion
¹/₂ Asian pear, or ¹/₂ kiwi fruit
1 chestnut, sliced
3 spring onions (scallions), sliced
50g/2oz/¹/₄ cup Korean chilli powder
120ml/4fl oz/¹/₂ cup fermented yellow bean sauce or light soy sauce
5ml/1 tsp sugar
1 red chilli, sliced

1 Make a deep cut across the base of the head of Chinese leaves and split it in two. Repeat this with the two halves, splitting them into quarters. Then place the quartered head in a bowl and cover it with water, adding 30ml/2 tbsp salt. Leave the quarters to soak for around 2 hours.

2 Drain the cabbage and sprinkle with the sea salt for the marinade, making sure to coat between the leaves. Leave to stand for 4 hours.

3 To make the seasoning, peel the radish and slice into fine strips. Peel the garlic cloves and finely chop into small pieces.

4 Cut the chives and *minari*, watercress or rocket into 5cm/2in lengths. Finely chop the ginger, onion and Asian pear or kiwi fruit. Combine the seasoning ingredients with 120ml/4fl oz/¹/₂ cup water.

5 Rinse the softened quarters of Chinese leaves in cold running water. Place in a large bowl and coat with the seasoning mixture, ensuring that the mixture gets between the leaves and that no leaf is left uncovered.

6 The outermost leaf of each quarter of cabbage will have softened and can be wrapped tightly around the other leaves to help the seasoning permeate throughout the whole.

7 Place the Chinese leaves in an airtight container. Leave to stand at room temperature for 5 hours, then leave in the refrigerator for 24 hours.

COOK'S TIP

Kimchi can be stored for up to 5 months in the refrigerator. The flavour may, by then, be too pungent for the vegetable pickle to be eaten raw, but at this stage it can be used to flavour cooked dishes.

Per portion Energy 73kcal/303kJ; Protein 3.6g; Carbohydrate 13.5g, of which sugars 12.9g; Fat 0.6g, of which saturates 0.1g; Cholesterol 0mg; Calcium 121mg; Fibre 5.1g; Sodium 383mg.

PAK CHOI KIMCHI

The pak choi green leaves that originated in China have been adopted all over Asia. In Korea they are used widely in making kimchi. This version is easy to prepare, with pumpkin adding sweetness and helping to marry the other flavours.

SERVES FOUR

INGREDIENTS
    8 small, white-stemmed pak choi
        (bok choy)
    15ml/1 tbsp sesame seeds, to garnish
For the stuffing
    250g/9oz pumpkin, peeled and
        seeded
    115g/4oz leeks, finely chopped
    1 garlic clove, crushed
    30ml/2 tbsp light soy sauce
    5ml/1 tsp grated fresh root ginger
    30ml/2 tbsp Korean chilli powder
    5ml/1 tsp sesame oil
    7.5ml/1½ tsp pine nuts, ground

1 Make sure the pak choi is fresh, crisp and bright. Reject any limp, bruised or broken pieces. Slice the pak choi in half lengthways. Rinse the pieces under running water, then drain and set aside.

2 Finely grate the pumpkin and place it in a bowl with the leeks and garlic.

3 Add the soy sauce, ginger, chilli powder, sesame oil, pine nuts and a pinch of salt. Mix thoroughly.

4 Place the pieces of pak choi in a serving bowl. Stuff the pumpkin mixture in between the leaves. Sprinkle any remaining stuffing over the top of the pak choi. Garnish with sesame seeds and serve.

COOK'S TIPS
• If pumpkin is not available, butternut squash can be used for this dish. To prepare the pumpkin or squash, discard the seeds, fibres and pith from the middle and cut off the thick peel. Then cut the flesh into chunks.
• A food processor can be used for speeding up preparation. Start by grinding the pine nuts as they are dry (a small bowl is ideal for this). Then chop the leeks, garlic and ginger together. Finally, use the grating blade for the pumpkin – or cheat and chop the vegetable finely instead.

Per portion Energy 77kcal/317kJ; Protein 6.1g; Carbohydrate 4.6g, of which sugars 3.9g; Fat 5.5g, of which saturates 0.6g; Cholesterol 0mg; Calcium 284mg; Fibre 4.2g; Sodium 519mg.

DICED WHITE RADISH KIMCHI

WHITE RADISH KIMCHI IS TRADITIONALLY EATEN AS THE AUTUMN EVENINGS START TO DRAW IN, AS IT HAS A SPICINESS THAT FORTIFIES AGAINST THE COLD. THE PUNGENT AROMAS AND TANGY FLAVOURS MAKE THIS ONE OF THE MOST POPULAR VARIETIES OF KIMCHI.

SERVES FOUR

INGREDIENTS

1.5kg/3½lb Chinese white radish, peeled
225g/8oz/2 cups coarse sea salt

For the seasoning

5ml/1 tsp sugar
75ml/5 tbsp Korean chilli powder
1 garlic clove, crushed
½ onion, finely chopped
3 spring onions (scallions), finely sliced
15ml/1 tbsp sea salt
5ml/1 tsp light soy sauce sauce
5ml/1 tsp fresh root ginger, peeled and finely chopped
22.5ml/4½ tsp light muscovado (brown) sugar

COOK'S TIP
Adjusting the seasoning makes a big difference to this dish. For extra kick, add a finely chopped red chilli to the seasoning, but be warned, this will make the dish extremely hot. Alternatively, blend half an onion in a food processor and add it to the seasoning to achieve a tangier taste and a subtle sweetness.

1 Cut the radish into 2cm/¾in cubes. Place in a bowl and coat with the sea salt. Leave for 2 hours, draining off any water that collects at the bottom of the bowl. Drain well at the end of salting.

2 Combine all the ingredients for the seasoning and mix well with the salted radish. Place the radish in an airtight container and seal. Leave at room temperature for 24 hours then chill.

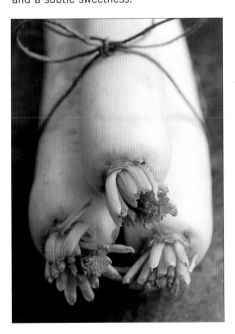

Per portion Energy 73kcal/302kJ; Protein 3.1g; Carbohydrate 14g, of which sugars 13.6g; Fat 0.8g, of which saturates 0.4g; Cholesterol 0mg; Calcium 81mg; Fibre 3.7g; Sodium 1203mg.

WHITE KIMCHI

THIS STUFFED CABBAGE VERSION MAY BE MORE TIME-CONSUMING AND AMBITIOUS TO PREPARE THAN MOST KIMCHI, BUT IT IS NEVERTHELESS A FIRM FAVOURITE. WITH AN ELEGANT APPEARANCE AND A SUBTLE REFINED FLAVOUR, THIS DISH IS REGARDED AS A LUXURIOUS ACCOMPANIMENT TO ANY MEAL.

3 For the stuffing, mix the red and green chillies, radish, spring onions, ginger, red dates and watercress in a bowl. Add the *taucheong*, sugar and garlic, then mix all the ingredients until they are thoroughly combined.

4 Rinse the cabbage and drain the leaves. Push the stuffing mixture in between the leaves, then place the stuffed halves into a bowl and pour over the kelp stock. Leave the cabbage to soak for a day at room temperature.

5 Remove the cabbage from the stock and slice each piece lengthways into quarters. Transfer to a bowl, cover and chill lightly. Garnish with pine nuts before serving.

SERVES FOUR

INGREDIENTS

1 white cabbage (Chinese cabbage)
100g/3¾oz salt
1 sheet dried kelp
½ white onion, finely grated or puréed
1 apple, thinly sliced
1 Asian pear, thinly sliced
1 red date, thinly sliced
20g/¾oz/2 tbsp pine nuts, ground

For the stuffing
2 red chillies, seeded and sliced
2 green chillies, seeded and sliced
200g/7oz Chinese white radish, peeled and finely sliced
50g/2oz spring onions (scallions), roughly chopped
15ml/1 tbsp grated fresh root ginger
2 red dates, seeded and sliced
40g/1½oz watercress or Korean *minari*, roughly chopped
15ml/1 tbsp *taucheong* (fermented soy bean paste)
scant 5ml/1 tsp sugar
5 garlic cloves, crushed

1 Cut the cabbage in half lengthways and place on a large dish. Sprinkle the salt over the cut surface. Spray the cabbage with water, then leave for 5 hours until the leaves have softened and lost their crispness.

2 Meanwhile bring 2.5 litres/4 pints/ 10 cups water to the boil in a pan and add the kelp. Reduce the heat slightly and simmer for 10 minutes, then strain the stock into a bowl and set it aside. Stir the onion, apple, Asian pear, red date and a pinch of salt into the kelp stock.

Per portion Energy 107kcal/446kJ; Protein 4.3g; Carbohydrate 13.8g, of which sugars 13.1g; Fat 4g, of which saturates 0.3g; Cholesterol 0mg; Calcium 122mg; Fibre 5.2g; Sodium 384mg.

STUFFED CUCUMBER KIMCHI

A CLASSIC SUMMER VARIETY OF KIMCHI. THE REFRESHING NATURAL SUCCULENCE OF CUCUMBER IS PERFECT ON A HOT, HUMID DAY. THE SPICINESS OF THE CHILLI IS NEUTRALIZED BY THE MOISTNESS OF THE CUCUMBER, AND THE COMBINED FLAVOURS INVIGORATE THE PALATE.

SERVES 4

INGREDIENTS
    15 small pickling cucumbers
    30ml/2 tbsp sea salt
    1 bunch Chinese chives
For the seasoning
    1 onion
    4 spring onions (scallions), thinly
      sliced
    75ml/5 tbsp Korean chilli powder
    15ml/1 tbsp light soy sauce
    10ml/2 tsp salt
    1 garlic clove, crushed
    7.5ml/1½ tsp grated fresh root ginger
    5ml/1 tsp sugar
    5ml/1 tsp sesame seeds

1 If the cucumbers are long, cut them in half widthways. Make two slits in a cross down the length of each cucumber or cucumber half, making sure not to cut all the way to the end. Coat thoroughly with salt and leave for 1 hour.

2 Cut the Chinese chives into 2.5cm/ 1in lengths, discarding the bulb.

3 Combine the onion and spring onions with the Chinese chives in a bowl. Add 45ml/3 tbsp of the chilli powder and add the soy sauce, salt, garlic, ginger, sugar and sesame seeds. Mix the ingredients thoroughly by hand, using plastic gloves to prevent the chilli powder from staining your skin. Alternatively, use a spoon and fork to fold the ingredients together.

4 Lightly rinse the cucumbers to remove the salt crystals. Coat with the remaining chilli powder and press the seasoning into the slits. Put the cucumber into an airtight container and leave at room temperature for 12 hours before serving.

COOK'S TIPS
• Cucumber *kimchi* can be stored in the refrigerator, although it is best eaten within two days.
• Traditional British cucumbers are not the best choice for this recipe – large smooth-skinned gherkins or ridge cucumbers are better. They have a firmer texture, with less watery flesh and are used for all types of pickles in European recipes. They are delicious with the spicy *kimchi* seasoning and they retain a refreshingly crisp texture.

Per portion Energy 32kcal/131kJ; Protein 2.5g; Carbohydrate 3.9g, of which sugars 3.4g; Fat 2.1g, of which saturates 0.2g; Cholesterol 0mg; Calcium 88mg; Fibre 1.4g; Sodium 2067mg.

VEGETABLE FRITTERS

THESE LIGHT AND CRUNCHY VEGETABLE FRITTERS ARE EQUALLY GOOD AS AN APPETIZER OR AS A QUICK SNACK ON THE GO. SIMPLE TO PREPARE AND EASY TO COOK, THEY ARE WONDERFULLY APPEALING AS THEY EMERGE GOLDEN BROWN FROM THE FRYING PAN.

SERVES FOUR

INGREDIENTS
    1 potato, thinly sliced
    1 small carrot, thinly sliced
    ½ small white onion, sliced
    ½ courgette (zucchini), thinly sliced
    1 red chilli, seeded and sliced
    salt and ground black pepper
    vegetable oil, for cooking
For the batter
    115g/4oz/1 cup plain (all-purpose)
        flour
    45ml/3 tbsp cornflour (cornstarch)
    1 egg, beaten
    5ml/1 tsp salt
For the dip
    30ml/2 tbsp dark soy sauce
    15ml/1 tbsp vegetable stock
    15ml/1 tbsp Chinese white
        radish, grated
    5ml/1 tsp vinegar
    5ml/1 tsp sesame seeds

1 To make the batter, sift the flour and cornflour into a bowl. Make a well in the middle and add the beaten egg with 250ml/8fl oz/1 cup water.

2 Blend the egg, water and salt with a wire whisk until smooth. Then gradually work in the flour mixture until it combines in a smooth batter. The batter should be thick enough to hold the vegetables together but it should still pour slowly from a ladle.

3 Place the potato, carrot, onion, courgette and chilli in a bowl. Mix them together well, then pour in the batter and mix it into the vegetables, adding a small amount of seasoning.

4 For the dip, mix the soy sauce, stock, white radish, vinegar and sesame seeds. Then set this aside to allow the flavours to mingle.

5 Heat a little vegetable oil in a frying pan or wok over a medium heat. Ladle three or four small portions of the fritter mixture into the pan (depending on the size of pan) and cook until they are set and golden brown underneath. Turn and cook the fritters on the second side until they are golden.

6 Drain the fritters on kitchen paper and keep hot in a warm oven or grill (broiler) compartment. Cook the remaining mixture in the same way.

7 Divide the dipping sauce among four small individual dishes. Serve the hot fritters on platters with the dishes of dipping sauce.

Per portion Energy 317kcal/1330kJ; Protein 6.7g; Carbohydrate 45.5g, of which sugars 5.3g; Fat 13.3g, of which saturates 1.9g; Cholesterol 48mg; Calcium 77mg; Fibre 2.7g; Sodium 1063mg.

PAN-FRIED KIMCHI FRITTERS

A CLASSIC APPETIZER AND POPULAR SNACK, THESE FRITTERS HAVE A CRISP GOLDEN COATING. THE CONTRAST OF THE CRUNCHY EXTERIOR AND SMOOTH FILLING MAKES FOR A DELICIOUS JUXTAPOSITION OF TEXTURES, AND THE DISH IS SERVED WITH A ZESTY SOY DIP TO HELP BRING OUT THE FLAVOURS.

SERVES TWO

INGREDIENTS

- 90g/3½oz cabbage *kimchi* (see page 29), finely chopped
- 1 potato
- a little milk (optional)
- 50g/2oz firm tofu, squeezed to remove excess water
- 25g/1oz/¼ cup plain (all-purpose) flour
- 1 egg, beaten
- 5ml/1 tsp crushed garlic
- 15ml/1 tbsp vegetable oil
- salt and ground black pepper

For the dip

- 45ml/3 tbsp light soy sauce
- 2.5ml/½ tsp sesame oil
- 5ml/1 tsp lemon juice

1 Gently squeeze the *kimchi* to remove any excess liquid. Boil the potato and mash it, adding a little milk if required.

2 Crumble the tofu into a bowl. Add the *kimchi*, potato, flour, egg, garlic and seasoning. Mix well and form spoonfuls of mixture into small round patties.

3 Coat a frying pan or wok with the oil and place over a medium heat. Add the patties and fry until golden brown on both sides. Drain on kitchen paper.

4 For the dip, mix the soy sauce, sesame oil and lemon juice, and then serve with the fritters.

Per portion Energy 206kcal/863kJ; Protein 8.4g; Carbohydrate 20.9g, of which sugars 3.8g; Fat 10.5g, of which saturates 1.8g; Cholesterol 105mg; Calcium 188mg; Fibre 1.9g; Sodium 583mg.

STEAMED TOFU AND CHIVE DUMPLINGS

THE SLIGHT SPICINESS AND DELICATE TEXTURE OF KOREAN CHIVES MAKE THEM A WONDERFUL INGREDIENT TO ADD TO THESE STUFFED, PAPER-THIN STEAMED DUMPLINGS, CALLED MANDU. HERE THE SUCCULENT FILLING IS MADE WITH TOFU, COMBINED WITH QUORN MINCE AND RICE WINE.

SERVES FOUR

INGREDIENTS
  30 dumpling skins
  1 egg, beaten
  spinach leaves to line steamer
For the filling
  3 spring onions (scallions),
    finely chopped
  3 garlic cloves, crushed
  5ml/1 tsp finely grated fresh
    root ginger
  5ml/1 tsp mirin or rice wine
  90g/3½oz/scant ½ cup
    Quorn mince
  90g/3½oz firm tofu
  90g/3½oz Korean chives, finely
    chopped
  ½ onion, finely chopped
  30ml/2 tbsp soy sauce
  30ml/2 tbsp sesame oil
  15ml/1 tbsp sugar
  15ml/1 tbsp salt
  10ml/2 tsp ground black pepper
For the dipping sauce
  60ml/4 tbsp dark soy sauce
  30ml/2 tbsp rice vinegar
  5ml/1 tsp Korean chilli powder

1 To make the dipping sauce, mix the soy sauce, rice vinegar and chilli powder in a small serving bowl.

2 For the filling, combine the chopped spring onions, garlic, ginger, mirin or rice wine and Quorn mince into a bowl. Leave to marinate for 15 minutes.

3 Drain off any excess liquid from the tofu then crumble it into a bowl. Season the filling mixture, then add the chopped chives with the tofu and remaining filling ingredients.

4 Take a dumpling skin and brush with a little beaten egg. Place a spoonful of the stuffing in the middle.

5 Fold into a half-moon shape, crimping the edges firmly to seal. Repeat with the other dumpling skins.

6 Cook over a pan of boiling water in a steamer lined with spinach leaves for 6 minutes. Alternatively, cook them in boiling water for 3 minutes. Arrange on a serving dish and serve with soy dipping sauce.

VARIATIONS
Almost any ingredient can be adapted for *mandu* fillings: beansprouts, courgettes (zucchini) and cabbage *kimchi* (see page 29) are favourites.

COOK'S TIPS
• Asian stores often stock dumpling skins and these are quick to use if you are in a rush, but they are not difficult to make if you have time. For 8 dumpling skins, sift 115g/4oz/1 cup plain (all-purpose) flour and 30ml/2 tbsp cornflour (cornstarch) together in a bowl and add 2.5ml/½ tsp salt. Pour in 50ml/2fl oz/¼ cup warm water and knead well until a smooth, elastic dough has formed. Cover the bowl with a damp dish towel and leave for 10 minutes. Place on a lightly floured surface and roll out the dough until paper-thin. Use a floured pastry (cookie) cutter or a sharp knife to cut the dough into circles roughly 7.5cm/3in in diameter.
• Dumplings can be cooked in a variety of ways. Steaming is the most popular, but grilling (broiling) and shallow-frying until golden brown also produce delicious results.

Per portion Energy 235kcal/982kJ; Protein 9.9g; Carbohydrate 26.1g, of which sugars 6.5g; Fat 10.8g, of which saturates 2.5g; Cholesterol 14mg; Calcium 208mg; Fibre 2.2g; Sodium 1054mg.

SWEET POTATO <u>WITH</u> ALMOND SYRUP

This simple yet interesting street dish, called MATANG, *is thought to have its origins in Chinese cooking. Deep-fried sweet potato is coated in a syrup containing almonds and sprinkled with black sesame seeds, creating a dish that is at once savoury and sweet.*

SERVES FOUR

INGREDIENTS

3 sweet potatoes, peeled
115g/4oz/½ cup light muscovado (brown) sugar
2 almonds, crushed
vegetable oil, for deep-frying
black sesame seeds, to garnish

1 Preheat the oven to 200°C/400°F/Gas 6. Cut the sweet potatoes into bitesize slices, then soak them in cold water for 15 minutes to help remove the starch. Drain, and place the potato slices on a baking sheet. Cook in the oven for 20 minutes, or until they have softened slightly. The potato slices should be parboiled rather than cooked through.

2 Put the sugar in a pan with 120ml/4fl oz/½ cup water. Simmer over a medium heat until it has formed a sticky syrup.

3 Remove the pan from the heat and add the crushed almonds.

4 Fill a wok or medium heavy pan one-third full of vegetable oil and heat over a high heat to 170°C/340°F, or when a small piece of bread dropped into the oil browns in 15 seconds.

5 Add the sweet potato. Deep-fry for about 5 minutes, or until golden brown, and then remove from the pan and drain any excess oil on kitchen paper.

6 Combine the potatoes with the syrup, coating each piece evenly. Transfer to a shallow serving dish and garnish with black sesame seeds before serving.

VARIATION
Create a more Western-shape fried potato by cutting the sweet potato into long thin strips, about 2.5cm/¼in thick.

Per portion Energy 667kcal/2819kJ; Protein 5g; Carbohydrate 124.4g, of which sugars 77.4g; Fat 20.2g, of which saturates 2.5g; Cholesterol 0mg; Calcium 115mg; Fibre 7.6g; Sodium 124mg.

SWEET CINNAMON PANCAKES

A CLASSIC STREET SNACK, THESE SOFT, SWEET PANCAKE TREATS ARE ADAPTED FROM A CLASSIC CHINESE RECIPE. THEY ARE QUICK AND EASY TO MAKE AND ARE ALWAYS POPULAR WITH CHILDREN. THEY ARE ENJOYED PARTICULARLY DURING THE WINTER, SERVED WARM ON A COLD DAY.

MAKES TEN

INGREDIENTS
- 15ml/1 tbsp sugar
- 5ml/1 tsp dried yeast
- 120ml/4fl oz/½ cup milk
- 175g/6oz/1½ cups plain (all-purpose) flour
- 50g/2oz/½ cup glutinous rice flour
- 2 tsp salt

For the filling
- 30ml/2 tbsp peanuts
- 60ml/4 tbsp sugar
- 5ml/1 tsp ground cinnamon

1 Pour 120ml/4fl oz/½ cup lukewarm water into a bowl and stir in the sugar. Sprinkle in the yeast and leave to stand, without stirring, for 5 minutes to allow the yeast to begin fermenting.

2 Sift the plain flour and rice flour together into a large mixing bowl. Add the salt, yeast liquid and milk, then mix the ingredients into a firm dough and knead this thoroughly on a lightly floured surface until it becomes smooth and elastic.

3 Replace the dough in the bowl, cover it with a board or a dish towel and leave at room temperature or in a warm place for about 3 hours, until risen and doubled in size.

4 To make the filling, grind the peanuts finely in a food processor then mix them with the brown and white sugars and the cinnamon.

5 Sprinkle a plate with a little flour. Divide the dough into ten portions. Flatten one piece on your hand, then make a depression in the centre with one finger. Place 30ml/2 tbsp filling on the middle of the dough and wrap the edges around to enclose the filling completely, shaping the dough back into a ball. Place on the plate. Repeat with the remaining dough and filling.

6 Pour a little vegetable oil into a frying pan and heat over a medium heat. Add a ball of dough and press it down with the back of a wooden spoon to flatten it into a round pancake. Prepare three or four at once (depending on the pan size). Fry on both sides until golden, then transfer to a warm plate. Keep hot in a warm oven while cooking the remaining pancakes. Serve warm.

Per portion Energy 119kcal/506kJ; Protein 4.9g; Carbohydrate 20.5g, of which sugars 2.7g; Fat 2.6g, of which saturates 0.9g; Cholesterol 35mg; Calcium 98mg; Fibre 0.7g; Sodium 34mg.

SOUPS

Korean soup is a versatile food, eaten as a snack, as an accompaniment to a main meal and as a nourishing dish in its own right. Often using doenjang soya bean paste, the typically light, clear soups are characterized by flavourings such as seaweed and white radish. Cold Radish Kimchi Soup, Spicy Potato and Courgette Soup and Wheat Noodles in Soya Bean Soup are examples of dishes that can be served either chilled during the warmer months or piping hot on colder days.

WHEAT NOODLES IN SOYA BEAN SOUP

STRANDS OF THIN WHEAT NOODLES TASTE GREAT IN A MILD AND DELICIOUSLY NUTTY CHILLED SOUP, MAKING AN IDEAL DISH FOR A HOT SUMMER'S DAY. THE ICED BROTH IS TOPPED WITH FRESH, APPETIZING STRIPS OF CUCUMBER AND WEDGES OF TOMATO.

SERVES FOUR

INGREDIENTS
185g/6½oz/1 cup soya beans
30ml/2 tbsp sesame seeds
300g/11oz thin wheat noodles
salt
1 cucumber, cut into thin strips
  and 1 tomato, cut into wedges,
  to garnish

VARIATION
For a quick and easy version of this dish use 250ml/8fl oz/1 cup unsweetened soya milk rather than the soaked soya beans. Simply add the ground sesame seeds to the soya milk and chill to make the soup.

COOK'S TIP
To separate the skins from the beans, place them in a bowl of cold water: the skins will float and can be skimmed off.

1 Soak the soya beans overnight. Rinse in cold water and remove the skins.

2 Toast the sesame seeds in a dry pan until lightly browned. Place the soya beans and sesame seeds in a food processor with 1 litre/1¾ pints/4 cups water and process until fine.

3 Strain through muslin (cheesecloth), collecting the liquid. Chill the soya and sesame milk in the refrigerator.

4 Bring a pan of water to the boil and cook the noodles, making sure they are well covered. When they are cooked, drain them and rinse them well in cold water.

5 Place a portion of the wheat noodles in each soup bowl, and pour over the chilled soya and sesame liquid. Garnish the bowls with strips of cucumber and tomato wedges, then season with salt and serve.

Per portion Energy 268kcal/1121kJ; Protein 20.1g; Carbohydrate 17.9g, of which sugars 3.4g; Fat 13.3g, of which saturates 1.7g; Cholesterol 0mg; Calcium 174mg; Fibre 8.7g; Sodium 6mg.

DUMPLING SOUP

THE SUCCULENT DUMPLINGS TASTE FANTASTIC IN THIS CLEAR SOUP. AS READY-TO-EAT DUMPLINGS ARE WIDELY AVAILABLE, THIS DISH IS REALLY SIMPLE TO MAKE AND A DELIGHT TO EAT, SERVED WARM FOR A QUICK SNACK OR LIGHT LUNCH.

SERVES TWO

INGREDIENTS
750ml/1¼ pints/3 cups vegetable stock
16 frozen dumplings
1 spring onion (scallion)
¼ green chilli
1 garlic clove, crushed
15ml/1 tbsp light soy sauce
salt and ground black pepper

COOK'S TIP
This dish is quick and easy to make, but if you have the time, you could make your own vegetable stock and dumplings. Try Steamed Tofu and Chive Dumplings on page 36 and the recipe for vegetable stock on page 25.

1 Thinly slice the spring onion and chilli, removing the seeds.

2 Place the stock in a pan and bring to the boil. Add the frozen dumplings, cover, and boil for 6 minutes.

3 Add the spring onion, chilli, garlic and soy sauce, to the stock already in the pan and boil for 2 minutes.

4 Season with salt and black pepper, leave to cool, then ladle into bowls and serve while still warm.

Per portion Energy 106kcal/445kJ; Protein 2g; Carbohydrate 12.6g, of which sugars 0.6g; Fat 6.1g, of which saturates 3.4g; Cholesterol 5mg; Calcium 30mg; Fibre 0.5g; Sodium 842mg.

WINTER KIMCHI SOUP

The spicy flavours of chilli and ginger in this chilled soup are uniquely warming on a cold winter's night. Traditionally, the soup was served with sweet potatoes.

SERVES FOUR

INGREDIENTS

3 Chinese white radishes, peeled
115g/4oz/½ cup salt
4 spring onions (scallions), shredded
1 garlic clove, sliced
115g/4oz fresh root ginger, sliced
2 red chillies, seeded and sliced
3 green chillies, seeded and sliced
1 Asian pear, peeled and diced
sugar syrup, to taste
10g/¼oz/1 tbsp pine nuts, to garnish

COOK'S TIP
To make a light sugar syrup, dissolve 225g/8oz/1 cup sugar in 600ml/ 1 pint/2½ cups water in a pan over a medium heat, stirring occasionally. Bring to the boil and boil for 2–3 minutes, until the syrup has reduced slightly. Take care not to allow the sugar to burn. Leave the syrup to cool. Store the syrup in an airtight jar in the refrigerator, where it will keep for up to 2 weeks. Alternatively, freeze the syrup in 50ml/2fl oz/¼ cup containers.

1 Place the Chinese white radishes in a bowl. Pour in 3.5 litres/6 pints/15 cups water and the salt, and leave them to soak overnight.

2 The next day, add the spring onions to the radishes in salt water and leave them to stand for 30 minutes.

3 Tie the garlic and ginger in a muslin (cheesecloth) bag and add to the radishes and spring onion with the red and green chillies. Cover and leave to stand for another day in the refrigerator.

4 Remove the radishes from the mixture, cut them into bitesize dice and then return the pieces to the soup. Remove and discard the garlic and ginger.

5 Add the pear to the soup, adding a little sugar syrup if it is too salty. Serve garnished with pine nuts.

COOK'S TIP
Peeled radishes are milder than unpeeled ones. To prepare a radish, slice off the roots and leaves, wash under cold running water and drain.

Per portion Energy 48kcal/198kJ; Protein 1.7g; Carbohydrate 5.9g, of which sugars 5.8g; Fat 2.1g, of which saturates 0.2g; Cholesterol 0mg; Calcium 37mg; Fibre 2g; Sodium 28mg.

COLD RADISH KIMCHI SOUP

THIS ICE-COLD SOUP IS NORMALLY SERVED AS AN ACCOMPANIMENT TO HOT MAIN DISHES. THE SPICY SEASONING AND TANGY KIMCHI CONTRASTS DELICIOUSLY WITH THE CHILLED BROTH.

SERVES EIGHT

INGREDIENTS

- 1 Chinese leaves (Chinese cabbage)
- 150g/5oz Chinese white radish, peeled and diced
- 50g/2oz/¼ cup salt
- 50g/2oz Korean chilli flakes
- 1 Asian pear, peeled and diced
- 2 cucumbers, finely sliced
- 75g/3oz watercress
- 75g/3oz spring onions (scallions), roughly sliced
- 10 garlic cloves, crushed
- 25g/1oz fresh root ginger, finely sliced
- 25g/1oz/3 tbsp pine nuts, to garnish

1 Slice the cabbage and cut the radish into cubes measuring about 3cm/1¼in. Place the vegetables in a large bowl. Add 250ml/8fl oz/1 cup water and the salt, and leave to stand for 1 hour.

2 Pour 2 litres/3½ pints/8¾ cups water into a very large large bowl. Tie the chilli flakes in a muslin (cheesecloth) bag, and then put it in the water.

3 Cover the bowl and set it aside until the water has taken on the colour and flavour of the chilli. Then, remove the bag and skim out any flakes that may have escaped from the bag and are left in the water.

4 Drain the cabbage and radish and add them to the chilli water. Leave to stand for 30 minutes.

5 Add a further 2 litres/3½ pints/8¾ cups water. Stir in the Asian pear, cucumbers, watercress, spring onions, garlic and ginger. Set the soup aside for 30 minutes to allow the flavours to develop and mingle.

6 Season the soup with a little salt, if required, then serve garnished with the pine nuts.

Per portion Energy 92kcal/382kJ; Protein 3.4g; Carbohydrate 8g, of which sugars 5.7g; Fat 5.4g, of which saturates 0.5g; Cholesterol 0mg; Calcium 67mg; Fibre 2.2g; Sodium 15mg.

COLD SUMMER CUCUMBER SOUP

Naturally cool and refreshing cucumber is sharpened with cider vinegar in this chilled soup, which is perfect for cooling everyone down at lunch on a hot summer day. It makes a great appetizer before any hot noodle or barbecue dish.

SERVES FOUR

INGREDIENTS

2 cucumbers
1 garlic clove
50g/2oz spring onions (scallions)
30ml/2 tbsp cider vinegar
30ml/2 tbsp sugar syrup
salt

1 Thinly slice the spring onions into long lengths, discarding the bulb. Peel and crush the garlic.

2 Combine 500ml/17fl oz/2 generous cups water with the garlic, spring onions (scallions), cider vinegar and sugar syrup (see Cook's Tip). Cover and leave to one side.

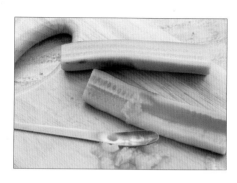

3 Peel the cucumbers, cut them in half, removing the seeds, then slice into thin strips. Add salt and leave for 10 minutes.

4 Add the previously prepared mix to the cucumber. Season to taste then ladle into bowls. Serve cold.

COOK'S TIP
For the sugar syrup, dissolve 225g/8oz/1 cup sugar in 600ml/1 pint/2½ cups water in a pan over a medium heat, stirring occasionally. Bring to the boil and leave for 2–3 minutes, until the syrup has reduced slightly. Take care not to let the sugar burn. Leave to cool before using.

Per portion Energy 40kcal/166kJ; Protein 0.8g; Carbohydrate 9.2g, of which sugars 9.1g; Fat 0.2g, of which saturates 0g; Cholesterol 0mg; Calcium 20mg; Fibre 0.6g; Sodium 30mg.

SPICY POTATO <small>AND</small> COURGETTE SOUP

*THIS KOREAN TAKE ON A TYPICAL WESTERN SOUP IS SEASONED WITH SPICES FOR A LIVELY
KICK. THE GOCHUJANG CHILLI PASTE ALSO HELPS TO THICKEN THE SOUP AND GIVE IT A SILKY
TEXTURE. THE ADDITION OF POTATOES MAKE IT A REALLY HEARTY AND FILLING MEAL IN A BOWL.*

SERVES TWO

INGREDIENTS

- 5ml/1 tsp salt
- 400g/14oz baby new potatoes, peeled
- 5ml/1 tsp sesame oil
- 15ml/1 tbsp Korean chilli powder
- 5ml/1 tsp *gochujang* chilli paste (see page 23)
- 1 garlic clove, crushed
- 115g/4oz Quorn mince
- 1 small courgette (zucchini), halved and sliced
- 1 red chilli, seeded and thinly sliced
- ½ small leek, thinly sliced
- 5ml/1 tsp sake
- 1 spring onion (scallion), shredded, to garnish

1 Fill a large pan with 750ml/1¼ pints/3 cups water and bring it to the boil. Add the salt and the potatoes.

2 Mix the sesame oil, chilli powder, *gochujang* paste and garlic with the Quorn mince until well combined. Add the seasoned mince mixture to the pan and boil for 5 minutes.

3 Add the courgette and boil for a further 3 minutes. Then add the chilli, leek and sake and boil for 2 minutes. Garnish with the spring onion.

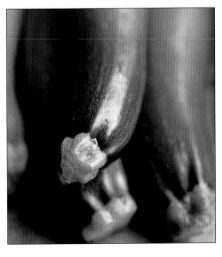

Per portion Energy 371kcal/1552kJ; Protein 18.6g; Carbohydrate 38.2g, of which sugars 5.6g; Fat 17.1g, of which saturates 5.3g; Cholesterol 35mg; Calcium 70mg; Fibre 4.1g; Sodium 73mg.

RICE & NOODLES

Rice and noodles form the backbone of nearly every meal in Korea. Rice, or bap, *is preferred in the sticky short and medium grain varieties and is traditionally cooked on its own, although additions such as beans, chestnuts and soya beansprouts are also popular. It is used to make delicious savoury Vegetable Porridge, piquant Ginseng and Red Date Rice, and sweet dishes such as Pumpkin Congee, a type of rice porridge. Noodles are also often used in chilled salads for hot days, in dishes such as Spicy Buckwheat Noodles.*

STIR-FRIED KIMCHI AND RICE

UBIQUITOUS KOREAN KIMCHI IS NORMALLY ENJOYED AS AN APPETIZER OR ACCOMPANIMENT, BUT THIS DISH TURNS IT INTO A MAIN COURSE. STIR-FRYING THE KIMCHI BRINGS OUT ITS NATURAL SWEETNESS, WHILE THE INCLUSION OF RICE BALANCES SOME OF THE CHILLI SPICINESS.

2 Add the cooked rice and mix it with the *kimchi* before adding the green pepper and sesame oil. Stir-fry for a further 5 minutes.

3 Divide the rice between two bowls and garnish with the chopped chives and a sprinkle of sesame seeds.

COOK'S TIP
Use scissors to chop chives and spring onions instead of a knife. Hold them in a bunch over a bowl and snip tiny slices.

SERVES TWO

INGREDIENTS
  45ml/3 tbsp vegetable oil
  5ml/1 tsp Korean chilli powder
  500g/1¼lb *kimchi*, cut into
    bitesize pieces
  200g/7oz/1 cup sticky rice, cooked
  ½ small green (bell) pepper, seeded
    and finely chopped
  15ml/1 tbsp sesame oil
For the garnish
  30ml/2 tbsp chopped chives
  15ml/1 tbsp sesame seeds

1 Heat a wok over a medium heat. Add the vegetable oil, chilli powder and *kimchi*. Stir-fry until lightly browned.

Per portion Energy 697kcal/2900kJ; Protein 13.2g; Carbohydrate 98g, of which sugars 17.6g; Fat 27.7g, of which saturates 3.5g; Cholesterol 0mg; Calcium 200mg; Fibre 7.3g; Sodium 23mg.

VEGETABLE PORRIDGE

WITH A TEXTURE SIMILAR TO RISOTTO, THIS DISH MAKES A POPULAR, FORTIFYING BREAKFAST.
BECAUSE IT USES SESAME OIL RATHER THAN BUTTER, IT IS LIGHTER THAT ITS ITALIAN EQUIVALENT
AND IS WIDELY REGARDED AS A NUTRITIOUS OPTION BY HEALTH-CONSCIOUS KOREANS.

SERVES TWO

INGREDIENTS
115g/4oz/⅔ cup short grain rice or
   pudding rice
1 dried shiitake mushroom
15ml/1 tbsp sesame oil
1 spring onion (scallion),
   finely chopped
1 small carrot, finely chopped
750ml/1¼ pints/3 cups
   vegetable stock
salt and ground black pepper
For the garnish
   2 quail's egg yolks
   sesame seeds

1 Soak the rice in cold water for
30 minutes, then drain and rinse well.

2 Soak the shiitake mushroom in warm
water for about 15 minutes, or until soft,
then chop finely, discarding the stalk.

3 Coat a pan with the sesame oil and
place on medium heat. Add the spring
onion, carrot, mushroom and a pinch of
salt and stir-fry briefly. Add the rice and
stir-fry for 1 minute to coat the grains.

4 Pour in the stock. Reduce the heat
when the stock simmers. Simmer the
mixture, stirring gently, until the porridge
has thickened to a smooth consistency.
Season with salt and pepper.

5 Spoon the porridge into bowls.
Garnish each portion with a quail's egg
yolk and a sprinkling of sesame seeds.

COOK'S TIP
Instead of the quail's egg yolk, finish the
porridge with a halved boiled egg, if
preferred. The result is different –
stirring in the uncooked yolk enriches the
porridge as the yolk lightly cooks in the
hot mixture – but it still tastes good.

VARIATION
This versatile dish can be recreated with
any vegetable – you could try celery and
courgette (zucchini) as an alternative.

Per portion Energy 310kcal/1292kJ; Protein 6.1g; Carbohydrate 57.8g, of which sugars 8.4g; Fat 6.1g, of which saturates 0.8g; Cholesterol 0mg; Calcium 49mg; Fibre 2.1g; Sodium 5mg.

PUMPKIN CONGEE

THE NATURAL SWEETNESS OF PUMPKIN IS EXCELLENT IN THIS POPULAR AUTUMNAL SNACK, WHICH IS SUITABLE BOTH AS AN ACCOMPANIMENT TO SAVOURY DISHES AND AS A DESSERT. DESPITE ITS HUMBLE ORIGINS AS A FARMER'S STAPLE, THIS CONGEE IS ENJOYED THROUGHOUT KOREAN SOCIETY.

SERVES TWO TO THREE

INGREDIENTS
  600g/1lb 6oz pumpkin, seeded,
    peeled and cut into chunks
  75g/3oz/⅔ cup sweet or glutinous
    rice flour
  30g/1¼oz/2 tbsp sugar
  5 chestnuts, cooked, peeled
    and crushed
  salt
For the garnish
  1 red date, seeded and finely sliced
    pine nuts

COOK'S TIP

Canned pumpkin pieces or purée can be used in this recipe. Cooked, puréed pumpkin freezes very well and is ideal for making dishes such as this one.

1 Place the pumpkin in a large pan and add just enough water to cover the pieces. Bring to the boil and simmer until the pumpkin is soft, then drain, reserving the cooking liquid. Cool the pumpkin slightly before blending it to a smooth paste in a food processor, adding a little of the reserved cooking water if it is very thick. Set aside.

2 Place the rice flour in a pan and stir in 200ml/7fl oz/scant 1 cup water. Cook over medium heat, stirring, until boiling and thickened.

3 Gradually stir in the pumpkin and sugar with a pinch of salt. Add the chestnuts. Simmer the congee briefly, stirring until it is smooth and creamy.

4 Ladle the congee into glass dishes or bowls and serve, decorated with sliced red date and pine nuts.

Per portion Energy 185kcal/781kJ; Protein 3.4g; Carbohydrate 41g, of which sugars 15g; Fat 1g, of which saturates 0.3g; Cholesterol 0mg; Calcium 77mg; Fibre 3.2g; Sodium 4mg.

MIUM CONGEE

ORIGINATING IN CHINA, THIS RICE PORRIDGE IS POPULAR ALL OVER ASIA. AS A MEDICINAL DISH, SERVED TO RESTORE STAMINA, MIUM IS TRADITIONALLY MADE USING ONLY RICE; HOWEVER, THE OTHER INGREDIENTS BRING AN UNFORGETTABLE FLAVOUR, ESPECIALLY WHEN FINISHED WITH A SWIRL OF SOY SAUCE.

SERVES ONE

INGREDIENTS
  50g/2oz/¼ cup short grain rice or
    pudding rice
  1 small piece ginseng root, halved
  25g/1oz dried seaweed
  1 dried shiitake mushroom
  2 red dates
  3 chestnuts, cooked and peeled
  30g/1¼oz leeks

1 Soak the rice in cold water for 30 minutes, then drain and rinse. Place the rice in a pan and add the ginseng, seaweed, shiitake mushroom, dates, chestnuts and leeks.

2 Pour in 1 litre/1¾ pints/4 cups water. Bring to the boil, reduce the heat and cover the pan.

3 Simmer for 20–30 minutes, stirring occasionally, until the rice has broken down and the congee is smooth and milky in consistency.

4 To serve, pour the mixture through a sieve (strainer) into a bowl and discard the flavouring ingredients.

COOK'S TIP
Try kelp or wakame seaweed – *dahima* or *miyuk* in Korean – in this dish. A dash of soy sauce makes a finishing touch.

Per portion Energy 238kcal/997kJ; Protein 4.9g; Carbohydrate 51.8g, of which sugars 2.8g; Fat 1.2g, of which saturates 0.2g; Cholesterol 0mg; Calcium 31mg; Fibre 1.9g; Sodium 4mg.

PINE NUT CONGEE

RICH AND NUTRITIOUS, PINE NUTS ARE VALUED IN KOREAN COOKING FOR THEIR DISTINCTIVE, SLIGHTLY FRAGRANT FLAVOUR. IN THIS DELICIOUS DISH THE PINE NUTS GIVE THE RICE A WOODY TASTE AND SUBTLE SWEETNESS AS WELL AS A PLEASING TEXTURE.

SERVES ONE

INGREDIENTS
  115g/4oz/⅔ cup short grain rice or
    pudding rice
  50g/2oz/⅓ cup pine nuts, ground,
    plus 6 pine nuts
  1 red date, seeded and thinly
    sliced, to garnish

1 Soak the rice in plenty of cold water for 30 minutes.

2 Drain the rice in a sieve (strainer) and rinse it well. Shake it thoroughly to get rid of excess water, then grind it to a powder in a food processor.

3 Place the ground pine nuts in a food processor. Pour in 200ml/7fl oz/ scant 1 cup water and process to a fine paste.

4 Place the ground rice in a pan with 750ml/1¼ pints/3 cups water and bring to the boil.

5 Reduce the heat, cover the pan and simmer for 20 minutes. The grains will break down and produce a milky congee.

6 Remove the pan from the heat and stir in the pine nuts. Serve garnished with the whole pine nuts and red date.

Per portion Energy 806kcal/3359kJ; Protein 16.1g; Carbohydrate 106.3g, of which sugars 14.5g; Fat 34.9g, of which saturates 2.3g; Cholesterol 0mg; Calcium 37mg; Fibre 1.7g; Sodium 3mg.

SOYA BEANSPROUT RICE

BLENDED THROUGH THE RICE, SOYA BEANSPROUTS IMPART A PLEASING CRUNCHINESS AND REFRESHING FLAVOUR, WHICH IS ENHANCED BY GARLIC, CHILLIES AND SPRING ONION. THIS DISH HAS THE REPUTATION OF BEING IRRESISTIBLE — IT IS IMPOSSIBLE TO REFUSE A SECOND HELPING.

SERVES FIVE

INGREDIENTS
- 200g/7oz/1 cup short grain rice
- 450g/1lb/2 cups soya beansprouts
- 1 garlic clove, crushed
- 5ml/1 tsp light soy sauce
- 15ml/1 tbsp sesame oil
- salt

For the sauce
- 1 garlic clove, crushed
- 2.5ml/½ tsp grated fresh root ginger
- 7.5ml/1½ tsp seeded and sliced jalapeño pepper
- 15ml/1 tbsp seeded and sliced red chilli
- 2.5ml/½ tsp sugar
- 45ml/3 tbsp light soy sauce
- 30ml/2 tbsp sesame seeds
- 1 spring onion (scallion), finely chopped
- 7.5ml/1½ tsp Korean chilli powder
- 45ml/3 tbsp finely chopped button (white) mushrooms

1 Soak the rice in cold water for 30 minutes, drain in a sieve (strainer) and then rinse it well.

2 Bring 750ml/1¼ pints/3 cups water to the boil in a pan and then add a pinch of salt.

3 Add the soya beansprouts to the pan and boil for 3 minutes. Drain the sprouts, reserving the cooking liquid and rinse.

4 Place the soya beansprouts in a bowl. Add the garlic, soy sauce, sesame oil and a pinch of salt. Mix and set aside.

5 Place the rice in a pan and pour in enough of the reserved cooking liquid to cover the rice by about 1cm/½in. Bring to the boil and cook for 5 minutes.

6 Add the soya beansprouts, reduce the heat and cook for a further 12 minutes, until all the water has evaporated.

7 Using a small dish, thoroughly combine the garlic, ginger, jalapeño pepper, chilli, sugar, soy sauce, sesame seeds, spring onion, chilli powder and button mushrooms.

8 To serve, divide the rice among serving bowls and top with the ginger and sesame seed sauce.

COOK'S TIP

Beans are easily sprouted at home. Mung beans are particularly simple and quick, as are soya beans and chickpeas. You simply need to soak them in water overnight, and then drain them and place in a jar. Cover with a cloth and keep in a shaded place at room temperature. Rinse twice a day to keep the beans moist and fresh.

Per portion Energy 233kcal/974kJ; Protein 7.2g; Carbohydrate 36.6g, of which sugars 3g; Fat 6.4g, of which saturates 0.9g; Cholesterol 0mg; Calcium 70mg; Fibre 1.9g; Sodium 860mg.

GINSENG AND RED DATE RICE

The mixture of rice and grains in this dish creates a pleasing appearance and deliciously complex flavour. The medicinal properties of ginseng have long been valued in Korea and this traditional ceremonial dish is renowned for increasing stamina and vitality.

SERVES FOUR

INGREDIENTS
115g/4oz/⅔ cup mixed grains
50g/2oz/¼ cup short grain rice or
    pudding rice
50g/2oz/¼ cup glutinous, sticky or
    pearl rice
50g/2oz/¼ cup brown rice
10 aduki or red beans
5 red dates
10 chestnuts, cooked and peeled
fresh ginseng root
salt

VARIATION
For a different combination, use short grain rice with the mixed grain selection.

1 Combine the grains, the three types of rice and the aduki or red beans in a bowl. Pour in cold water to cover and leave to soak for 2 hours. Drain the rice mixture through a sieve (strainer) and rinse thoroughly under cold water. Transfer the rice and beans to a large pan.

2 Discard the seeds from the dates and slice the dates into small pieces. Halve the chestnuts and slice the ginseng root into two pieces (do not slice the ginseng if it is a small piece).

3 Add the dates, chestnuts and ginseng to the rice and mix together thoroughly. Pour in water to cover the ingredients by about 1cm/½in. Add a pinch of salt. Bring to the boil and cook for five minutes, then reduce the heat and simmer for a further 15 minutes or until all the water has evaporated. Stir thoroughly and serve.

COOK'S TIPS
• Mixed grain rice is made from a mixture of brown rice, sweet rice, wild rice, barley, hulled millet, green peas, yellow peas, black-eyed beans (peas), kidney beans and red beans. It is available from Korean or Japanese food stores.
• Glutinous rice is a sticky rice. There are many types of short grain rice, including Western pudding and risotto rice. Pearl rice sometimes refers to short, or round, grain rice. Asian and wholefood stores stock many varieties.

Per portion Energy 383kcal/1609kJ; Protein 8.3g; Carbohydrate 84.4g, of which sugars 2.1g; Fat 1.5g, of which saturates 0.2g; Cholesterol 0mg; Calcium 33mg; Fibre 2.1g; Sodium 4mg.

SPICY BUCKWHEAT NOODLES

THIS CHILLED NOODLE SALAD, CALLED BIBIM NAENGMYUN, *IS IDEAL FOR A SUMMER LUNCH DISH AND IS NOT TIME-CONSUMING TO MAKE. THE COOL TEMPERATURE OF THE BUCKWHEAT NOODLES CONTRASTS WITH THE SPICINESS OF THE DRESSING, AND ASIAN PEAR ADDS A DELICIOUS SWEETNESS.*

SERVES TWO

INGREDIENTS
- 90g/3½oz *naengmyun* buckwheat noodles
- 1 hard-boiled egg
- ½ cucumber
- ½ Asian pear
- ice cubes, to serve

For the sauce
- 30ml/2 tbsp *gochujang* chilli paste
- 5ml/1 tsp Korean chilli powder
- 30ml/2 tbsp sugar
- 10ml/2 tsp sesame oil
- 1 garlic clove, finely chopped
- 2.5ml/½ tsp soy sauce
- 5ml/1 tsp sesame seeds

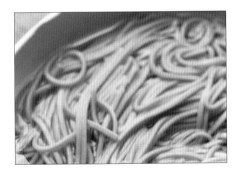

1 Cook the noodles in a large pan of boiling water for 5 minutes. Drain them, and then rinse two or three times in cold water until the water runs clear. Chill for 30 minutes.

2 Slice the hard-boiled egg in half. Seed the cucumber and slice it into long, thin matchstick strips. Peel and core the Asian pear and slice it into fine matchstick strips.

COOK'S TIP
Be sure to use a large pan with plenty of water when cooking *naengmyun* noodles, as they contain a lot of starch so will stick to the pan and each other easily. Add a few drops of oil while cooking to help prevent the water from frothing up and boiling over; this also helps to keep the noodles separate when they are first drained.

3 In a large bowl combine all the ingredients for the sauce and blend them together well. Arrange the noodles in the centre of a large serving platter. Pour over the sauce and then sprinkle with the pear and cucumber strips. Place the egg on the top and add ice cubes to the plate before serving.

Per portion Energy 337kcal/1421kJ; Protein 9.4g; Carbohydrate 58.3g, of which sugars 25.1g; Fat 9g, of which saturates 1.3g; Cholesterol 105mg; Calcium 52mg; Fibre 3.3g; Sodium 133mg.

VEGETABLE
SIDE DISHES

Korea's high mountain slopes provide a plentiful and varied array of wild vegetables, which are the inspiration for many classic dishes, such as Vegetable Buckwheat Crêpe with Mustard Dip, and Stuffed Aubergine with Rice Wine and Ginger. The Korean table also features a host of smaller dishes to accompany the main courses, known as namul. *These can be made from any available vegetable, such as Shiitake Mushroom Namul, Cucumber Namul or Soya Beansprout Namul.*

PAN-FRIED CHILLI PARSNIP <u>AND</u> SHIITAKE MUSHROOMS

THIS DISH HAS ITS ROOTS IN THE TEMPLES OF KOREA, ALTHOUGH THIS CONTEMPORARY VERSION ADDS MORE SPICES AND SEASONING THAN THE ORIGINALS. THE NATURAL SWEETNESS OF THE PARSNIPS IS BALANCED BY THE SPICINESS OF THE DRESSING.

SERVES FOUR

INGREDIENTS
   150g/5oz parsnips, finely sliced
   a little vegetable oil
   115g/4oz fresh shiitake
      mushrooms
   salt
   15ml/1 tbsp pine nuts, ground,
      to garnish
   sesame oil, to season
For the sauce
   45ml/3 tbsp *gochujang* chilli paste
   5ml/1 tsp Korean chilli powder
   15ml/1 tbsp maple syrup
   5ml/1 tsp sugar
   5ml/1 tsp soy sauce
   5ml/1 tsp sesame oil

1 Place the parsnips in a bowl and add a little sesame oil and salt. Coat the slices evenly. Set aside for 10 minutes.

2 For the sauce, mix the chilli paste and powder, maple syrup, sugar, soy sauce and sesame oil with a little water.

3 Heat a frying pan and add a little vegetable oil. Sauté the finely sliced parsnips until they are softened and lightly browned. Then transfer the parsnips to a bowl and add enough of the chilli sauce to coat them well.

4 Discard the stalks from the shiitake mushrooms and spoon the remaining chilli sauce into the caps.

5 Return the sautéed parsnips to the pan, with their sauce, and then add the mushrooms.

6 Cook the parsnip and mushroom mixture over low heat, allowing the chilli mixture to fully infuse the vegetables and form a sticky glaze. Then add more of the *gochujang* chilli paste if necessary.

7 When the vegetables are cooked and the liquid has reduced, transfer them to a serving dish, season with sesame oil and sprinkle with ground pine nuts.

Per portion Energy 86kcal/362kJ; Protein 2.3g; Carbohydrate 10.4g, of which sugars 6.4g; Fat 4.4g, of which saturates 0.5g; Cholesterol 0mg; Calcium 26mg; Fibre 2.1g; Sodium 106mg.

STUFFED AUBERGINE <u>WITH</u> RICE WINE <u>AND</u> GINGER SAUCE

THE TASTY QUORN MINCE FILLING COMPLEMENTS THE CREAMY TEXTURE OF THE BRAISED AUBERGINE BEAUTIFULLY, AND THE WHOLE DISH IS INFUSED WITH THE FLAVOURS OF RICE WINE AND GINGER; AN ADDITIONAL FIERY KICK IS SUPPLIED BY CHILLIES.

SERVES TWO

INGREDIENTS

 2 aubergines (eggplants)
 1 egg
 25ml/1½ tbsp vegetable oil
 1 sheet dried seaweed
 90g/3½oz/scant ½ cup
   Quorn mince
 15ml/1 tbsp *mirin* or rice wine
 15ml/1 tbsp dark soy sauce
 1 garlic clove, crushed
 5ml/1 tsp sesame oil
 1 red chilli, seeded and
   shredded
 1 green chilli, seeded
   and shredded
 salt and ground black pepper
 steamed rice, to serve
For the sauce
 30ml/2 tbsp mirin or rice wine
 30ml/2 tbsp dark soy sauce
 5ml/1 tsp fresh root ginger, peeled
   and grated

COOK'S TIP
If you would like to reduce the heat of the dish, then avoid using the red chilli and just use the green chilli.

1 Clean the aubergines, and cut into slices about 2.5cm/1in thick.

2 Make two cross slits down the length of each aubergine slice, making sure that you don't cut all the way through. Then sprinkle each one with a little salt and set aside.

3 Beat the egg and season with a pinch of salt. Coat a frying pan with 10ml/2 tsp vegetable oil and heat over medium heat.

4 Add the beaten egg and make a thin omelette, browning gently on each side. Remove the omelette from the pan and cut it into thin strips. Wait until it is cool and then chill in the refrigerator.

5 Heat the remaining vegetable oil over high heat. Cut the seaweed into strips and stir fry with the Quorn, *mirin* or rice wine, soy sauce and garlic. Once cooked, drizzle the beef with the sesame oil.

6 Place the chillies in a bowl. Add the egg strips and mix with the Quorn. Rinse the aubergines and stuff each slice with a little of the mince mixture.

7 Place all the ingredients for the sauce into a frying pan, add 200ml/7fl oz/ scant 1 cup of water and salt to taste, and heat over medium heat. Once the sauce is blended and bubbling add the stuffed aubergine slices. Spoon the sauce over the aubergines and simmer for 15 minutes, or until the aubergines are soft and the skin has become shiny. Transfer to a shallow dish and serve with steamed rice.

Per portion Energy 273kcal/1134kJ; Protein 14.3g; Carbohydrate 5.9g, of which sugars 5.3g; Fat 19.9g, of which saturates 5.2g; Cholesterol 122mg; Calcium 42mg; Fibre 4g; Sodium 1145mg.

VEGETABLE BUCKWHEAT CRÊPE WITH MUSTARD DIP

This historic dish celebrates the range of vegetables native to Korea. The ingredients form a medley of tastes and colours, all wrapped in a buckwheat crêpe. Slicing the crêpe before serving creates bitesize pieces reminiscent of Japanese maki rolls.

SERVES FOUR

INGREDIENTS
    50g/2oz *minari* or watercress
    50g/2oz/½ cup beansprouts
    400g/14oz Chinese white radish,
      finely sliced
    25g/1oz dried shiitake mushrooms
    1 garlic clove, crushed
    5ml/1 tsp spring onion (scallion),
      finely chopped
    5ml/1 tsp soy sauce
    5 red dates, finely chopped
    vegetable oil, for cooking
    1 small carrot
For seasoning
    sesame oil
    sesame seeds
    salt
    sugar
For the buckwheat crêpe
    115g/4oz/1 cup buckwheat flour
    50g/2oz/1 cup wholemeal
      (whole-wheat) flour
    1 egg white, lightly whisked
    5ml/1 tsp salt
For the dip
    15ml/1 tbsp Korean mustard powder
      or German mustard
    15ml/1 tbsp vinegar
    7.5ml/1½ tbsp sugar
    2.5ml/½ tsp soy sauce

1 Bring a pan of water to the boil and add a pinch of salt. Add the watercress and beansprouts, bring back to the boil, then immediately drain them and rinse under cold water. Drain thoroughly, place in a bowl and season with a little sesame oil. Sprinkle lightly with sesame seeds, then set aside.

COOK'S TIPS
• When turning crêpes, slide a spatula under the edge to loosen. Then move the spatula as close to the centre as possible and flip to the other side.
• To keep crêpes warm, cover with plastic wrap (clear film) and a thick towel.

2 Prepare another pan of salted boiling water. Add the Chinese radish and boil for about 10 minutes, until cooked and tender. Drain, place the radish in a bowl and season with salt, sesame oil and sesame seeds, then set aside.

3 Soak the shiitake mushrooms in warm water to cover for about 15 minutes, until they have softened.

4 Drain and thinly slice the mushrooms, discarding their stalks. Mix them with the garlic, spring onions and soy sauce. Season with a pinch each of salt and sugar, a little sesame oil and a sprinkling of sesame seeds.

5 Heat a frying pan or wok. Add a little vegetable oil and stir-fry the mushrooms until they are cooked and tender, then remove from the pan and set aside.

6 To make the crêpes, sift the buckwheat and wholemeal flours into a bowl. Add the egg white and a little water, stirring gently.

7 Continue to stir and add more water to make a smooth batter. Leave to rest for 30 minutes before cooking.

8 Heat a pan and pour in a little vegetable oil. Tilt the pan to coat in oil, then pour in a ladleful of batter. Tilt the pan to spread the batter thinly and cook for 30 seconds, until set and browned.

9 Turn the crêpe and cook on the second side. Then remove from the pan and place on a plate. Cover loosely with foil and keep hot in a warm oven. Cook the remaining batter to make additional crêpes.

10 Place a little of each vegetable and some chopped dates in each crêpe and roll up. Slice into bitesize pieces and arrange on a serving platter.

11 To make the mustard dip, mix the mustard powder, vinegar and sugar with the soy sauce and 15ml/1 tbsp water. Transfer to individual dishes and serve with the crêpes.

Per portion Energy 167kcal/699kJ; Protein 6.3g; Carbohydrate 34.9g, of which sugars 2.8g; Fat 1.2g, of which saturates 0.2g; Cholesterol 0mg; Calcium 71mg; Fibre 3g; Sodium 410mg.

WHITE RADISH NAMUL

THIS SUBTLE DISH BLENDS THE SWEETNESS OF WHITE RADISH WITH A DELICIOUS NUTTY AFTERTASTE.
BLANCHING THE WHITE RADISH SOFTENS IT, LEAVING IT WITH A SILKY TEXTURE.

SERVES TWO

INGREDIENTS
400g/14oz Chinese white radish,
  peeled
50g/2oz leek, finely sliced
20ml/4 tsp sesame oil, plus extra
  for drizzling
5ml/1 tsp salt
60ml/4 tbsp vegetable oil
½ red chilli, seeded and finely
  shredded, to garnish

1 Slice the radish into 5cm/2in matchstick lengths. Blanch in a pan of boiling water for 30 seconds. Drain, and gently squeeze to remove any excess water. Pat dry with kitchen paper.

2 Mix the leek with the sesame oil and salt in a large bowl.

3 Sauté the radish in the vegetable oil for 1 minute. Add the leeks and sauté for a further 2 minutes. Garnish with the chilli and a drizzle of sesame oil.

Per portion Energy 137kcal/565kJ; Protein 1.8g; Carbohydrate 4.5g, of which sugars 4.3g; Fat 12.5g, of which saturates 1.8g; Cholesterol 0mg; Calcium 45mg; Fibre 2.4g; Sodium 1005mg.

SPINACH NAMUL

USING THE STEMS AS WELL AS THE LEAVES OF THE SPINACH GIVES A SUBTLE CRUNCH TO THIS DISH.
THE HINT OF BITTERNESS IN THE SPINACH IS BALANCED BY THE SALTY SOY SAUCE.

SERVES TWO

INGREDIENTS
500g/1¼lb spinach
60ml/4 tbsp dark soy sauce
2 small garlic cloves, crushed
20ml/4 tsp sesame oil
2.5ml/½ tsp rice wine
20ml/4 tsp sesame seeds
30ml/2 tbsp vegetable oil
salt

1 Trim the ends of the spinach stalks. Cut the leaves and stalks into 10cm/4in lengths. Blanch the spinach in a pan of lightly salted water for approximately 30 seconds. Drain the spinach, and rinse well under cold running water.

2 Mix the soy sauce, garlic, sesame oil and rice wine together in a large bowl. Add the spinach and thoroughly coat the leaves and stems with the seasoning mixture. In a dry pan lightly toast the sesame seeds until they are golden brown, then set aside.

3 Heat the vegetable oil in a frying pan or wok, and sauté the spinach over a high heat for 20 seconds. Transfer to a serving dish and garnish with the toasted sesame seeds before serving.

Per portion Energy 293kcal/1208kJ; Protein 10.1g; Carbohydrate 7.4g, of which sugars 6.1g; Fat 24.8g, of which saturates 3.2g; Cholesterol 0mg; Calcium 499mg; Fibre 6.2g; Sodium 2488mg.

SHIITAKE MUSHROOM NAMUL

IN THIS TEMPTING NAMUL DISH THE DISTINCTIVE TASTE OF SESAME OIL EMPHASIZES THE RICH FLAVOUR OF THE SHIITAKE MUSHROOMS. THE LATTER ARE SAUTÉED TO ACCENTUATE THEIR EARTHY TASTE.

SERVES TWO

INGREDIENTS

12 dried shiitake mushrooms, soaked in warm water for about 30 minutes until softened
10ml/2 tsp sesame seeds
2 garlic cloves, crushed
30ml/2 tbsp vegetable oil
½ spring onion (scallion), finely chopped
10ml/2 tsp sesame oil
salt

1 When the soaked shiitake mushrooms have reconstituted and become soft, drain and slice them, discarding the stems, and then place them in a bowl. Add the sesame seeds, crushed garlic and a pinch of salt, and blend the ingredients together.

2 Coat a frying pan or wok with the vegetable oil and place over high heat. Add the seasoned mushroom slices and quickly stir-fry them, so that they soften slightly but do not lose their firmness.

3 Remove from the heat and stir in the spring onion and sesame oil. Transfer to a shallow dish and serve.

COOK'S TIP
It is important that the shiitake mushrooms are drained thoroughly to ensure that their dark colour does not overwhelm the dish. Having drained them, then squeeze the mushrooms gently to remove all the excess liquid, and finally pat them dry with kitchen paper.

Per portion Energy 167kcal/689kJ; Protein 2.2g; Carbohydrate 1.1g, of which sugars 0.2g; Fat 17.2g, of which saturates 2.2g; Cholesterol 0mg; Calcium 38mg; Fibre 1.2g; Sodium 4mg.

BRAISED SHIITAKE MUSHROOM <u>AND</u> ONION

IN THIS DISH, THE EARTHY FLAVOURS OF THE MUSHROOMS ARE BALANCED BY THE NATURAL SWEETNESS OF THE ONION AND GARLIC. A KOREAN STAPLE FOR ANY DINNER TABLE.

SERVES TWO TO THREE

INGREDIENTS
  10 fresh shiitake mushrooms
  ½ white onion, finely diced
  5 garlic cloves, crushed
  1 spring onion (scallion),
    shredded
  5ml/1 tsp sesame seeds
For the sauce
  60ml/4 tbsp dark soy sauce
  15ml/1 tbsp sesame oil
  10ml/2 tsp maple syrup

1 Discard the stalks from the shiitake mushrooms and cut each cap in half.

2 Boil 350ml/12fl oz/1½ cups water. Add the soy sauce, sesame oil, maple syrup, mushrooms, onion and garlic.

3 Reduce the heat under the pan and simmer until the mushrooms are tender and the cooking liquid has reduced to form a rich sauce.

4 Transfer to a dish and serve sprinkled with spring onion and sesame seeds.

COOK'S TIP
Substitute the shiitake mushrooms with field (portabello), brown cap (cremini) or button (white) mushrooms.

Per portion Energy 117kcal/489kJ; Protein 3.5g; Carbohydrate 14.9g, of which sugars 13g; Fat 5.3g, of which saturates 0.8g; Cholesterol 0mg; Calcium 40mg; Fibre 2.2g; Sodium 1103mg.

CUCUMBER NAMUL

THIS SAUTÉED DISH RETAINS THE NATURAL SUCCULENCE OF THE CUCUMBER, WHILE ALSO INFUSING THE RECIPE WITH A PLEASANTLY REFRESHING HINT OF GARLIC AND CHILLI.

SERVES TWO

INGREDIENTS
200g/7oz cucumber
15ml/1 tbsp vegetable oil
5ml/1 tsp spring onion (scallion),
  finely chopped
1 garlic clove, crushed
5ml/1 tsp sesame oil
sesame seeds, and seeded and
  shredded red chilli, to garnish
salt

COOK'S TIP
You can adapt this dish and tone
down the hot chilli garnish by
substituting the red chilli for a milder
green chilli.

1 Thinly slice the cucumber and place the slices in a colander. Sprinkle with salt, then leave to stand for about 10 minutes. Then drain off any excess liquid and transfer the cucumber to a clean bowl.

2 Coat a frying pan or wok with the vegetable oil, and heat it over a medium heat. Add the spring onion, garlic and cucumber, and quickly stir-fry together.

3 Remove from the heat, add the sesame oil and toss lightly to blend the ingredients. Place in a shallow serving dish and garnish with the sesame seeds and shredded chilli before serving.

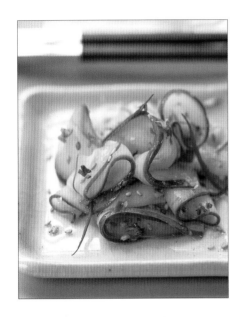

Per portion Energy 74kcal/304kJ; Protein 0.8g; Carbohydrate 1.7g, of which sugars 1.6g; Fat 7.1g, of which saturates 0.9g; Cholesterol 0mg; Calcium 20mg; Fibre 0.7g; Sodium 4mg.

SOYA BEANSPROUT NAMUL

THE DELICATE SPICINESS OF THE RED CHILLI AND NUTTY FLAVOUR OF THE SESAME OIL CREATE A TANTALIZING DISH. CRISPY SOYA BEANSPROUTS CAN BE REPLACED WITH MUNG BEANSPROUTS.

SERVES TWO

INGREDIENTS
300g/11oz/generous 1 cup soya
  beansprouts
60ml/4 tbsp vegetable oil
2/3 red chilli, seeded and
  sliced
1 baby leek, finely sliced
10ml/2 tsp sesame oil
salt

VARIATION
It is easy to sprout beansprouts at home.

1 Wash the soya beansprouts, and trim the tail ends. Cover them with a light sprinkling of salt, and leave them to stand for 10 minutes.

2 Bring a pan of water to the boil, and add the beansprouts. Cover and boil for 3 minutes, then drain.

3 Place a frying pan or wok over medium heat and add the vegetable oil.

4 Add the soya beansprouts, and sauté gently for 30 seconds. Add the chilli and leek, and stir-fry together so that the ingredients are thoroughly blended.

5 Transfer to a shallow dish and then drizzle with a little sesame oil before serving the *namul*.

Per portion Energy 282kcal/1167kJ; Protein 5.2g; Carbohydrate 7.5g, of which sugars 4.4g; Fat 26g, of which saturates 3.2g; Cholesterol 0mg; Calcium 42mg; Fibre 3.4g; Sodium 9mg.

SHREDDED LEEK WITH SESAME

THIS SIMPLE VEGETABLE DISH IS A CLASSIC AND SOMETIMES INDISPENSABLE ACCOMPANIMENT TO MORE HEAVY MAIN COURSE DISHES. THE SPICY CHILLI FLAVOUR IS GREAT FOR CLEANSING THE PALATE.

2 Meanwhile, make the dressing. Put the Korean chilli powder, sesame oil, crushed garlic and cider vinegar in a bowl and mix together well.

3 Add the sugar and stir well until it dissolves into the chilli, oil and vinegar mixture.

4 Add the sesame seeds and season to taste with a little salt.

5 Drain the leeks, discarding all the water and place them in a serving bowl.

SERVES THREE TO FOUR

INGREDIENTS
    250g/9oz leeks or spring onions
      (scallions)
    15ml/1 tbsp Korean chilli powder
    10ml/2 tsp sesame oil
    1 garlic clove, crushed
    5ml/1 tsp cider vinegar
    5ml/1 tsp sugar
    10ml/2 tsp sesame seeds
    salt

1 Finely shred the leeks or spring onions diagonally with a sharp knife and place in a large bowl. Pour in cold water and add a quantity of ice, then leave the leeks to soak for about 5 minutes.

6 Pour the dressing over the leeks and toss well before serving.

Per portion Energy 58kcal/242kJ; Protein 2g; Carbohydrate 4.5g, of which sugars 2.7g; Fat 3.8g, of which saturates 0.6g; Cholesterol 0mg; Calcium 39mg; Fibre 1.6g; Sodium 3mg.

SWEET LOTUS ROOT

THE ROOT OF THE LOTUS FLOWER HAS A UNIQUE FLAVOUR AND A CLEAN, CRISP TASTE. HISTORICALLY, THIS SPECIALITY WAS EATEN BY THE KING AS A DESSERT, BRAISED WITH SUGAR RATHER THAN SOY AS HERE.

SERVES TWO TO THREE

INGREDIENTS
    15ml/1 tbsp cider vinegar
    300g/11oz lotus root, peeled
    60ml/4 tbsp soy sauce
    30ml/2 tbsp sugar
    45ml/3 tbsp maple syrup
    10ml/2 tsp sesame oil
    sesame seeds, to garnish

3 Return the slices to the rinsed-out pan and add just enough water to cover them. Add the soy sauce. Bring to the boil and cook for 20 minutes, by which time the lotus root should have taken on the colour of the soy sauce.

4 Add the sugar and maple syrup, then reduce the heat and simmer for about 30 minutes. Mix in the sesame oil, coating the lotus root slices carefully. Transfer to a serving dish and garnish with a sprinkle of sesame seeds.

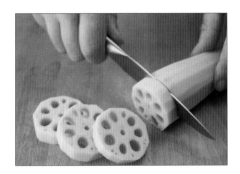

1 Pour 750ml/1¼ pints/3 cups water into a bowl and add the vinegar. Cut the lotus root into slices about 1cm/½in thick and place them in the vinegar water. Leave to soak for about 30 minutes, then drain. Be careful not to leave the lotus root in the water for too long or it will begin to turn black.

2 Bring 750ml/1¼ pints/3 cups water to the boil in a pan and add the lotus root. Boil for 2 minutes and then drain the lotus root and rinse the slices thoroughly under cold water.

COOK'S TIPS
• Once peeled fresh lotus root will discolour very quickly. Treat it in the same way you would an apple, ensuring that it is soaked in the acidulated water as soon as it is peeled to slow down this process.
• If possible use a mature lotus root for this recipe, as the starchy quality of the larger roots will be ideal for absorbing the flavours during the cooking process. Smaller lotus roots are often eaten raw and are delicious in salads.

Per portion Energy 131kcal/555kJ; Protein 1.2g; Carbohydrate 28.3g, of which sugars 28.1g; Fat 2.2g, of which saturates 0.3g; Cholesterol 0mg; Calcium 54mg; Fibre 1.1g; Sodium 1525mg.

SALADS & TOFU

Korean salads are eaten both as an accompaniment to a main course, such as Black Beans with Sweet Soy, or as dishes in their own right. Salads known as sangchae are tangy and crunchy, made with vegetables coated in a spicy dressing, like White Radish Sangchae and Korean Chive Sangchae. Tofu is a versatile soya beancurd used mainly for pan-fried, stewed or blanched dishes. Each method creates a different flavour, from the creamy texture of Stuffed Pan-fried Tofu, to the smoky richness of Blanched Tofu with Soy Dressing.

GREEN LEAF SALAD <u>IN</u> CHILLI DRESSING

SERVED AS AN ACCOMPANIMENT TO MAIN DISHES, THE SANGCHI IN THIS RECIPE ADDS A HINT OF BITTERNESS WHILE THE SHARP SPICINESS OF THE DRESSING GIVES A REFRESHING EDGE. A VARIETY OF GREEN SALAD LEAVES CAN BE USED IN THIS RECIPE, DEPENDING ON WHAT IS IN SEASON.

SERVES TWO TO THREE

INGREDIENTS
- 250g/9oz green salad leaves or Korean *sangchi*
- 115g/4oz leeks, finely sliced
- 1 white onion, finely sliced
- 2 green chillies, seeded and finely sliced
- 1 red chilli, seeded and finely sliced
- 15ml/1 tbsp sesame seeds, to garnish

For the dressing
- 5ml/1 tsp pine nuts, ground
- 15ml/1 tbsp Korean chilli powder
- 5ml/1 tsp sesame oil
- 1 garlic clove, crushed
- 30ml/2 tbsp light soy sauce
- 30ml/2 tbsp vegetable stock or water

1 Tear the leaves or *sangchi* into bitesize pieces. Mix the leeks, onion and green and red chillies.

2 For the salad dressing, mix the pine nuts with the chilli powder, sesame oil, garlic, soy sauce and stock or water in a bowl.

3 Stir the dressing gently, allowing the flavours to mingle, and then add the chillies, onion and leeks.

4 Place the green leaves or *sangchi* in a salad bowl and pour over the dressing. Toss the salad, garnish with sesame seeds and serve.

Per portion Energy 54kcal/224kJ; Protein 2.5g; Carbohydrate 4.1g, of which sugars 4g; Fat 3.2g, of which saturates 0.4g; Cholesterol 0mg; Calcium 58mg; Fibre 1.7g; Sodium 719mg.

CHINESE CHIVE AND ONION SALAD

THIS LIVELY SALAD IS A COMBINATION OF CRUNCHY SALAD LEAVES AND CABBAGE WITH A CHILLI POWDER AND SOY DRESSING. IT IS DELICIOUS SERVED ON ITS OWN AS A VEGETABLE DISH OR AS A PLEASANT ACCOMPANIMENT TO BIGGER DISHES.

SERVES TWO TO THREE

INGREDIENTS
  50g/2oz Chinese chives
  1 thin wedge Chinese leaves (Chinese cabbage), finely sliced
  1 thin slice red cabbage, finely sliced
  ¼ white onion, finely sliced
For the dressing
  15ml/1 tbsp soy sauce
  7.5ml/1½ tbsp Korean chilli powder
  7.5ml/1½ tbsp sesame seeds
  7.5ml/1½ tbsp sesame oil
  5ml/1 tsp cider vinegar
  5ml/1 tsp lemon juice
  5ml/1 tsp sugar
  1 garlic clove, crushed

1 Trim both ends off the Chinese chives and cut them into 5cm/2in long pieces.

2 Soak the onion, and the red cabbage and Chinese leaves, separately in two bowls of iced water for about 5 minutes, to soften the flavour of the cabbage.

3 Drain the onion and cabbage, then combine them with the chives in a serving dish and mix thoroughly.

4 For the dressing, combine the soy sauce, chilli powder, sesame seeds and oil, vinegar, lemon juice, sugar and garlic in a bowl. Mix the ingredients.

5 Drizzle the dressing over the chive mixture and serve.

Per portion Energy 47kcal/197kJ; Protein 1.7g; Carbohydrate 6.2g, of which sugars 5.7g; Fat 1.9g, of which saturates 0.3g; Cholesterol 0mg; Calcium 53mg; Fibre 1.8g; Sodium 362mg.

WHITE RADISH SANGCHAE

The red chilli and sesame oil dressing adds an understated spiciness and nutty aftertaste to this healthy dish. The white radish, also known as daikon, is a commonly used ingredient in Asian cooking and is valued for its medicinal properties.

SERVES TWO

INGREDIENTS

225g/8oz Chinese white radish, peeled
½ red chilli, shredded, and 1.5ml/
¼ tsp sesame seeds, to garnish
For the marinade
5ml/1 tsp cider vinegar
2.5ml/½ tsp sugar
1.5ml/¼ tsp salt
7.5ml/1½ tsp lemon juice
2.5ml/½ tsp Korean chilli powder

VARIATIONS
• The radish takes on the red colour of the chilli powder, but for an interesting alternative replace the chilli powder with 2.5ml/½ tsp wasabi. This will give the radish a green tint and a sharper taste.
• Make an alternative sesame oil marinade with 2.5ml/½ tsp sesame oil 2.5ml/½ tsp vegetable oil, 120ml/ 4fl oz/½ cup white wine vinegar, 50g/2oz/¼ cup sugar, 1.5ml/¼ tsp salt and a pinch of pepper.

1 Cut the radish into thin strips approximately 5cm/2in long.

2 To make the marinade, mix the vinegar, sugar, salt, lemon juice and chilli powder together in a small bowl, and ensure that the ingredients are thoroughly blended.

3 Place the radish in a bowl, and add the marinade. Leave to marinate for 20 minutes, then place in the refrigerator until the dish has chilled thoroughly.

4 Mix well again, then garnish with the shredded red chilli pepper and the sesame seeds before serving.

Per portion Energy 22kcal/91kJ; Protein 1g; Carbohydrate 3.2g, of which sugars 3.2g; Fat 0.7g, of which saturates 0.2g; Cholesterol 0mg; Calcium 27mg; Fibre 1.1g; Sodium 209mg.

CUCUMBER SANGCHAE

THE REFRESHING, SUCCULENT TASTE OF THIS SIMPLE SALAD MAKES A PERFECT ACCOMPANIMENT FOR A MAIN MEAL ON A HOT SUMMER'S NIGHT. SMALL PICKLING CUCUMBERS ARE THE BEST FOR THIS DISH; THEY ARE NOT AS WATERY AS THE LARGER SPECIMENS AND THEY DO NOT REQUIRE PEELING.

SERVES FOUR

INGREDIENTS
  400g/14oz pickling or salad
    cucumber
  30ml/2 tbsp salt
For the dressing
  2 spring onions (scallions)
  2 garlic cloves
  5ml/1 tsp cider vinegar
  5ml/1 tsp salt
  2.5ml/½ tsp Korean
    chilli powder
  10ml/2 tsp toasted sesame seeds
  10ml/2 tsp sesame oil
  5ml/1 tsp *gochujang* chilli paste
  10ml/2 tsp sugar

1 Cut the cucumber lengthways into thin slices and put into a colander. Sprinkle with the salt, mix well and leave for 30 minutes.

2 Place the cucumber slices in a damp dish towel and gently squeeze out as much of the water as possible.

3 Finely slice the spring onions into thin strips and place in a large bowl.

4 Crush the garlic and add to the spring onions. Add the vinegar, salt and chilli powder, and combine. Sprinkle in the toasted sesame seeds and mix in the sesame oil, chilli paste and sugar.

5 Blend the cucumber with the dressing and arrange on a plate.

6 Garnish with sesame seeds and chill before serving.

tion Energy 105kcal/432kJ; Protein 3.3g; Carbohydrate 9.2g, of which sugars 7.4g; Fat 6.2g, of which saturates 0.9g; Cholesterol 0mg; Calcium 78mg; Fibre 2.2g; Sodium 1973mg.

KOREAN CHIVE SANGCHAE

THE KOREAN CHIVE HAS A GARLIC NUANCE IN BOTH TASTE AND AROMA. THE LEAVES HAVE A SOFT, GRASSLIKE TEXTURE. THIS DISH IS A TASTY ALTERNATIVE TO A CLASSIC SHREDDED SPRING ONION SALAD.

SERVES TWO

INGREDIENTS
    200g/7oz fresh Korean or
      Chinese chives
    1 green chilli, seeded and
      finely sliced
    10ml/2 tsp sesame seeds,
      to garnish
For the seasoning
    30ml/2 tbsp dark soy sauce
    2 garlic cloves, crushed
    10ml/2 tsp Korean chilli powder
    10ml/2 tsp sesame oil
    10ml/2 tsp sugar

1 Clean the chives, then trim off the bulbs and discard. Slice roughly into 4cm/1½ in lengths. Combine with the chilli in a bowl.

2 To make the seasoning, mix the soy sauce, garlic, chilli powder, sesame oil and sugar together, and then add it to the bowl with the chives and chilli. Mix until well coated, then chill.

3 Garnish with sesame seeds and serve. The chives can be attractively arranged in alternating layers laid at right angles.

COOK'S TIP
Korean chives are available in most Asian markets in 225g/½lb or 450g/1lb bundles. When shopping for these chives, try to select those that are bright green with a crisp texture.

VARIATION
For a traditional alternative use 150g/5oz shredded spring onion (scallion) in place of the chives, and add 15ml/1 tbsp cider vinegar and 15ml/1 tbsp soy sauce to the seasoning.

Per portion Energy 105Kcal/434kJ; Protein 4.3g; Carbohydrate 7g, of which sugars 6.7g; Fat 6.7g, of which saturates 0.9g; Cholesterol 0mg; Calcium 196mg; Fibre 2.3g; Sodium 1196mg.

SPINACH KIMCHI SALAD

THIS APPETIZING SUMMER SALAD IS SIMPLE TO MAKE AND IS A PERFECT ACCOMPANIMENT FOR ANY NOODLE DISH. UNLIKE TRADITIONAL KIMCHI, THIS IS NOT PRESERVED AND SO THE TASTE IS LIGHTER.

SERVES TWO TO THREE

INGREDIENTS

500g/1¼lb spinach
1 leek, finely sliced
2 mild onions, finely sliced
For the dressing
15ml/1 tbsp glutinous rice
90ml/6 tbsp Korean chilli powder
  (40g/1½oz in weight)
8 spring onions, finely sliced
30ml/2 tbsp light soy sauce
1 green chilli, seeded and finely
  chopped
1 red chilli, seeded and finely chopped
3 garlic cloves, crushed
5ml/1 tsp grated fresh root ginger

1 Slice the spinach leaves into large pieces, rinse under cold running water, then drain well and set aside.

2 Place the rice in a medium pan. Add 50ml/2fl oz/¼ cup water and bring to the boil over a high heat. Simmer for about 20 minutes, until the liquid turns milky. Add the chilli powder, spring onions, soy sauce and chillies. Mix thoroughly and remove from the heat. Then add the garlic and the ginger.

3 Toss the leek and onions with the spinach in a large serving dish. Pour over the dressing and toss the salad. Serve immediately.

Per portion Energy 112kcal/468kJ; Protein 10.8g; Carbohydrate 9.7g, of which sugars 5g; Fat 3.4g, of which saturates 0.5g; Cholesterol 8mg; Calcium 405mg; Fibre 5.9g; Sodium 807mg.

BLACK BEANS WITH SWEET SOY

SIMPLE TO MAKE, AND POPULAR AS AN ACCOMPANIMENT, THIS IS AMONG THE OLDEST OF TRADITIONAL DISHES AND IS A STAPLE OF THE CUSTOMARY KOREAN TABLE. THE BLACK BEANS HAVE A SWEET, NUTTY TASTE THAT IS WELL MATCHED BY THE SALTY TANG OF SOY SAUCE.

SERVES TWO TO THREE

INGREDIENTS

300g/11oz/2 cups canned black
  beans, drained
120ml/4fl oz/½ cup maple
  syrup
30ml/2 tbsp sugar
100ml/3½fl oz/scant ½ cup light
  soy sauce
5ml/1 tsp sesame seeds,
  to garnish

1 Rinse the beans, then drain them.

2 Bring 750ml/1½pints/3 cups water to the boil in a pan and add the beans. Boil the beans for 5 minutes, by which time any odour from them should have disappeared. Drain the beans and rinse out the pan.

3 Bring 450ml/¾ pint/scant 2 cups water to the boil in the pan. Add the beans and maple syrup.

4 Boil for 3 minutes, then add the sugar and soy sauce.

5 Reduce the heat under the pan and simmer over low heat, until the liquid has reduced to form a thick, rich sauce.

6 Remove from the heat and leave to cool. Transfer the cooled beans to a dish and garnish with sesame seeds before serving.

VARIATION
If you liquidize this tasty recipe, its sweet and salty flavours make it a delicious additional ingredient for a vegetable stir fry or rice dish.

Per portion Energy 275kcal/1166kJ; Protein 7.8g; Carbohydrate 61.1g, of which sugars 47.8g; Fat 1.5g, of which saturates 0.2g; Cholesterol 0mg; Calcium 94mg; Fibre 5.8g; Sodium 2840mg.

BRAISED TOFU

TOFU IS A VERY POPULAR DISH IN KOREA. THE INGREDIENTS IN THE SAUCE PROVIDE A RANGE OF TASTES: SWEET, SALTY, NUTTY AND SPICY, AND REDUCING THE SAUCE DURING COOKING FORMS A STICKY GLAZE FOR THE DICED TOFU THAT IS QUITE IRRESISTIBLE.

SERVES TWO TO THREE

INGREDIENTS
    1 block firm tofu, diced
    250ml/8fl oz/1 cup
      vegetable stock
    45ml/3 tbsp soy sauce
    1 sheet dried kelp
    15ml/1 tbsp honey
    1 garlic clove, crushed
    ½ white onion, finely chopped
    1 green chilli, seeded and sliced
    1 red chilli, seeded and sliced
    15ml/1 tbsp Korean chilli
      powder
    5ml/1 tsp sesame seeds, to
      garnish

1 Cut the tofu into 1cm/½in cubes and place in a pan. Add 250ml/8fl oz/1 cup cold water, the vegetable stock and soy sauce.

2 Chop the dried kelp into strips and add to the pan.

3 Stir in the honey and garlic, then bring to the boil. Cover and boil for 5 minutes.

4 Add the onion, chillies and chilli powder. Reduce the heat and simmer for a further 10 minutes, until the liquid has reduced to a small amount of sauce.

5 Transfer the mix from the pan to a serving dish, garnish with a small sprinkling of sesame seeds and serve while still hot.

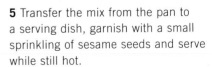

Per portion Energy 118kcal/490kJ; Protein 8.2g; Carbohydrate 14g, of which sugars 8.8g; Fat 3.7g, of which saturates 0.4g; Cholesterol 0mg; Calcium 385mg; Fibre 1.9g; Sodium 1076mg.

VEGETABLE AND TOFU CAKE WITH MUSTARD DIP

THIS DISH IS FILLED WITH A MOUTHWATERING BLEND OF TASTES AND TEXTURES, YET IS REMARKABLY SIMPLE TO PREPARE. THE CONTRAST BETWEEN THE DELICATE TEXTURE OF THE TOFU AND THE CRUNCHINESS OF THE MANGETOUTS IS DELIGHTFUL, AND THE SESAME SEEDS ADD A HINT OF NUTTINESS. EATEN WITH THE MUSTARD DIP, IT IS PERFECT AS A SNACK OR AS A SIDE DISH.

SERVES TWO

INGREDIENTS

    1 block firm tofu
    1 carrot, finely chopped
    115g/4oz mangetouts (snow peas),
       sliced
    3 eggs
    5ml/1 tsp sake or *mirin*
    10ml/2 tsp salt
    5ml/1 tsp grated fresh root
       ginger
    5ml/1 tsp sesame oil
    5ml/1 tsp sesame seeds
    ground black pepper
    vegetable oil, for greasing
       mould
For the mustard dip
    45ml/3 tbsp Dijon mustard
    15ml/1 tbsp sugar syrup
       (see below)
    7.5ml/1½ tsp soy sauce
    30ml/2 tbsp rice vinegar
    salt
To make sugar syrup
    1 part white sugar to 2 parts water
    (see Cook's Tip)

1 Bring a large pan of salted water to the boil. Add the block of tofu and then bring it back to the boil.

2 Use a large fish slice, metal spatula, or sieve (strainer) to remove and drain the tofu from the pan.

3 Crumble the block of tofu on to a piece of muslin (cheesecloth), and then squeeze it to drain off any excess water.

4 Bring a fresh batch of water to the boil and blanch the carrot for 1 minute.

5 Add the mangetouts, bring back to the boil and then drain the vegetables. The vegetables should be slightly cooked but retain their crunchy texture.

6 Beat the eggs and sake or *mirin* together briefly, then add them to the crumbled tofu.

7 Mix in the mangetouts and carrots, ginger, sesame oil and sesame seeds. Season with a little black pepper and mix well.

8 Grease a 18cm/7in mould with a little oil. Pour the mixture into the mould and place in a steamer. Lay a piece of foil over the top of the mould, to keep steam out and steam over boiling water for 20 minutes, until the mixture is set and firm.

9 Meanwhile, for the dip, mix the mustard, syrup, soy sauce and vinegar. Season with a little salt. Mix thoroughly and pour into two small serving bowls.

10 Slide a metal spatula between the tofu and the mould. Cover with a serving plate and then invert both mould and plate. Remove the mould and serve the tofu sliced, with the dipping sauce.

COOK'S TIP
To make sugar syrup, dissolve 1 part white sugar in 2 parts water over a low heat.

Stir until the sugar has dissolved, then bring to the boil for 1 minute. Remove from the heat and leave to cool. Store the syrup in a screw-top jar in the refrigerator for up to 2 weeks. You can also freeze it in ice cube trays.

Per portion Energy 320kcal/1334kJ; Protein 23g; Carbohydrate 16.4g, of which sugars 14.9g; Fat 18.7g, of which saturates 3.7g; Cholesterol 285mg; Calcium 662mg; Fibre 3.8g; Sodium 657mg.

BLANCHED TOFU WITH SOY DRESSING

THE SILKY CONSISTENCY OF THE TOFU ABSORBS THE DARK SMOKY TASTE OF THE SOY DRESSING IN THIS RICH AND FLAVOURFUL DISH. TOFU HAS A NUTTY QUALITY THAT BLENDS AGREEABLY WITH THE SALTY SWEETNESS OF THE SOY SAUCE AND THE HINTS OF GARLIC AND SPRING ONION.

SERVES TWO

INGREDIENTS
    2 blocks firm tofu
    salt
For the dressing
    10ml/2 tsp finely sliced spring
      onion (scallion)
    5ml/1 tsp finely chopped
      garlic
    60ml/4 tbsp dark soy sauce
    10ml/2 tsp chilli powder
    5ml/1 tsp sugar
    10ml/2 tsp sesame seeds

1 Mix the spring onion and garlic with the soy sauce, chilli powder, sugar and sesame seeds. Leave to stand for a few minutes.

2 Meanwhile, bring a large pan of water to the boil, and add a pinch of salt. Place the whole blocks of tofu in the water, being careful not to let them break apart.

3 Blanch the tofu for 3 minutes. Remove and place on kitchen paper to remove any excess water.

4 Transfer the tofu to a plate, and cover with the dressing. Serve, slicing the tofu as desired.

COOK'S TIP
Koreans traditionally eat this dish without slicing the tofu, preferring instead to either eat it directly with a spoon or pick it apart with chopsticks. It may be easier, however, to slice it in advance if you are serving it as an accompanying dish.

Per portion Energy 160kcal/669kJ; Protein 16.1g; Carbohydrate 6.7g, of which sugars 5.6g; Fat 7.8g, of which saturates 0.9g; Cholesterol 0mg; Calcium 954mg; Fibre 0.1g; Sodium 2144mg.

STUFFED PAN-FRIED TOFU

THIS IS AN EASY ACCOMPANIMENT FOR A MAIN COURSE, OR A GREAT APPETIZER. SQUARES OF FRIED TOFU STUFFED WITH A BLEND OF CHILLI AND CHESTNUT GIVE A PIQUANT JOLT TO THE DELICATE FLAVOUR. THE TOFU HAS A CRISPY COATING, SURROUNDING A CREAMY CENTRE, WITH A CRUNCHY FILLING.

SERVES TWO

INGREDIENTS
    2 blocks firm tofu
    30ml/2 tbsp light soy sauce
    5ml/1 tsp sesame oil
    2 eggs
    7.5ml/1½ tsp cornflour
      (cornstarch)
    vegetable oil, for shallow-frying
For the filling
    2 green chillies, finely chopped
    2 chestnuts, finely chopped
    6 garlic cloves, crushed
    10ml/2 tsp sesame seeds

1 Cut the two blocks of tofu into 2cm/¾in slices and then cut each slice in half. Place the tofu slices on pieces of kitchen paper to blot and absorb any excess water.

2 Mix together the soy sauce and sesame oil. Transfer the tofu slices to a plate and coat them with the soy sauce and oil mixture. Leave to marinate for 20 minutes. Meanwhile, put all the filling ingredients into a bowl and combine them thoroughly. Set aside.

3 Beat the eggs in a shallow dish. Add the cornflour and whisk until well combined. Take the slices of tofu and dip them into the beaten egg mixture, ensuring an even coating on all sides.

VARIATION
Alternatively, you can serve the tofu with a light soy dip instead of the spicy filling.

4 Place a frying pan or wok over a medium heat and add the vegetable oil. Add the tofu slices to the pan and sauté, turning over once, until they are golden brown.

5 Once cooked, make a slit down the middle of each slice with a sharp knife, without cutting all the way through. Gently stuff a large pinch of the filling into each slice, and serve.

Per portion Energy 291kcal/1213kJ; Protein 23g; Carbohydrate 7.8g, of which sugars 1.3g; Fat 19.1g, of which saturates 3.4g; Cholesterol 209mg; Calcium 1014mg; Fibre 0.8g; Sodium 88mg.

SWEETS, CAKES & DRINKS

Sweet dishes are uncommon in Korea, and when they do feature they tend to be served with tea rather than as a dessert at the end of a meal. The fluffy Sweet Rice Balls are popular, as are the Three-colour Ribbon Cookies, which contain crushed pumpkin, apricot and seaweed. Iced desserts, like Persimmon Sorbet in Ginger Punch, are perfect for hot and humid summer days, while sweet drinks are fruity and delicately spiced, such as a Persimmon and Walnut Punch.

POACHED PEAR <u>WITH</u> PEPPERCORNS

*FOR THIS DISH, CALLED BAESUK, ASIAN PEARS ARE GENTLY POACHED UNTIL TENDER IN LIQUID
SWIMMING WITH BLACK PEPPERCORNS AND SLICED GINGER. IT IS SWEET, BUT ITS LIGHT
SPICINESS MAKES FOR A CLEANSING AND PLEASANT END TO A MEAL.*

SERVES FOUR

INGREDIENTS
    2 Asian pears
    20 black peppercorns
    10g/¼oz fresh root ginger, peeled
      and sliced
    25g/1oz/2 tbsp sugar
    pine nuts, to decorate

1 Peel and core the Asian pears with
a sharp knife. Then cut each one into
six pieces.

COOK'S TIP
When choosing Asian pears at the
market, pick those that are most
even in shape, firm and free of
any soft spots.

2 Press two or three peppercorns into
the smooth outer surface of each piece.

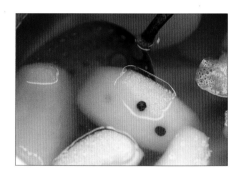

3 Place 750ml/1¼ pints/3 cups water in
a large pan and add the ginger. Bring to
the boil and cook for 10 minutes, or
until the flavour of the ginger has
suffused the water. Add the sugar and
then the pears. Reduce the heat, and
simmer for 5 minutes, or until the pears
have softened.

4 Transfer the fruit and liquid to a bowl.
Cool, remove the sliced ginger and
place the bowl in the refrigerator to chill
for a while.

5 Place three pieces of pear in a bowl
for each person. Pour over the poaching
liquid and decorate with pine nuts.

VARIATION
Asian pears are crisp and mild, whereas
European pears tend to have a more
aromatic and buttery flavour. If Asian
pears are not available, then Conference
pears can be used in their place. They
should be cored and used whole – one
per person – rather than sliced.

Per portion Energy 60kcal/253kJ; Protein 0.3g; Carbohydrate 15.4g, of which sugars 15.4g; Fat 0.1g, of which saturates 0g; Cholesterol 0mg; Calcium 12mg; Fibre 1.7g; Sodium 3mg.

SWEET BEANS ON ICE FLAKES

FOR THIS REFRESHING, CHILLED DESSERT, UNIQUE TO KOREA, CRUNCHY ICE FLAKES ARE COATED WITH A PURÉE OF RED BEANS AND MAPLE SYRUP AND THEN TOPPED WITH FRESH FRUIT. THIS IS UNQUESTIONABLY THE MOST POPULAR CHOICE FOR A HOT SUMMER'S DAY IN KOREA.

SERVES TWO

INGREDIENTS

    75g/3oz/½ cup red kidney beans,
      soaked overnight
    115g/4oz/generous ½ cup sugar
    5ml/1 tsp salt
    30ml/2 tbsp maple syrup
    ice cubes
    30ml/2 tbsp condensed milk
    90ml/6 tbsp milk
    1 kiwi fruit, sliced
    2 strawberries

1 Place the red kidney beans in a pan, cover with water and bring to the boil. Boil fast for 10 minutes, then simmer until the beans have softened. Drain and leave to cool, then roll them between the palms of your hands to remove the skins.

2 Put the peeled beans, sugar, salt and maple syrup into a food processor or blender and purée together to a fine paste. Put the puréed beans into a pan and simmer them until the paste has reduced to the consistency of a custard. Cool, then chill.

3 Use an ice crusher, food processor or blender to crush the ice into flakes (you will need 2 litres/3½ pints/8 cups of ice flakes) and transfer to a serving bowl.

4 Mix the condensed milk and milk in a jug (pitcher) and pour over the ice flakes in the bowl. Pour the bean paste over the top and decorate with the kiwi fruit and strawberries before serving.

VARIATIONS
A variety of fruits can be used depending on what is available or in season. Blueberries and raspberries both make delicious alternatives.

Per portion Energy 462kcal/1968kJ; Protein 11.4g; Carbohydrate 105.1g, of which sugars 88.4g; Fat 2.5g, of which saturates 1.2g; Cholesterol 6mg; Calcium 145mg; Fibre 7g; Sodium 1063mg.

PERSIMMON SORBET IN GINGER PUNCH

THE SWEET, AUTUMNAL FLAVOUR OF RIPE PERSIMMON GIVES THIS DESSERT A WONDERFULLY MELLOW TASTE. THE RICH, CREAMY SORBET SITS IN A BOWL OF PUNCH WHERE THE AROMATIC QUALITY OF THE FRUIT IS OFFSET BY THE INVIGORATING PEPPERY TASTE OF THE GINGER.

SERVES FOUR

INGREDIENTS
    300g/11oz persimmon purée
    75g/3oz dextrose or glucose
    10ml/2 tsp caster (superfine) sugar
    30ml/2 tbsp lemon juice
    Persimmon and walnut punch, to
        serve (see page 94)

COOK'S TIPS
• Dextrose is another name for glucose. This is available in powder form from health food shops or among speciality sweeteners and sugars.
• The sorbet can also be made in an ice cream maker, following the manufacturer's instructions.

1 Heat the persimmon purée in a pan over a low heat. Add the dextrose and use a whisk to stir it into the purée.

2 Add the sugar and bring to the boil. Once the mixture begins to bubble pour into a bowl, and leave to cool.

3 Stir in the lemon juice and chill the mixture thoroughly in the refrigerator, for about 10 hours.

4 Turn the freezer to the fast freeze setting, following the manufacturer's instructions. Transfer the mixture to a shallow freezer container.

5 Freeze the mixture, removing the container and stirring every 30 minutes or so to break up ice crystals as they form. The sorbet should be smooth and creamy.

6 To serve, place a scoop of sorbet in each bowl and pour over the ginger and persimmon punch.

Per portion Energy 109kcal/461kJ; Protein 0.3g; Carbohydrate 28.3g, of which sugars 28.3g; Fat 0.1g, of which saturates 0g; Cholesterol 0mg; Calcium 14mg; Fibre 1.1g; Sodium 4mg.

SWEET RICE <u>WITH</u> RED DATES

Traditionally used for ancestral memorial services, birthdays and weddings, this sweet cake is now enjoyed to celebrate any occasion. The red dates have a rich fruity flavour that permeates the rice, creating a sweet, appetizing dessert.

SERVES FOUR

INGREDIENTS
- 400g/14oz/2 cups glutinous rice
- 115g/4oz/½ cup brown sugar
- 8 cooked chestnuts, finely chopped
- 8 dried red dates, seeded and chopped
- 15ml/1 tbsp sesame oil
- 30ml/2 tbsp raisins
- 5ml/1 tsp ground cinnamon
- pine nuts
- salt

1 Soak the rice in plenty of cold water for 20 minutes. Drain the rice and place it in a heavy pan or a rice cooker.

2 Add the brown sugar and 200ml/7fl oz/scant 1 cup water to the pan. Stir all the ingredients well.

COOK'S TIPS
- If you are cooking on the type of electric cooker that retains heat, when the water boils, transfer it to another ring on the lowest setting to prevent the rice from cooking too quickly and sticking to the bottom of the pan.
- Rice cookers are relatively inexpensive to buy, and are particularly useful for cooking Korean recipes which always include rice. The cookers are thermostatically controlled and very useful for preventing burning. To use a rice cooker for this recipe, follow the manufacturer's instructions and cook until the rice is fully cooked and the liquid has been fully absorbed.

3 Add the chestnuts, dates, sesame oil and raisins to the rice. Add a little of the cinnamon and a pinch of salt. Add water until it covers the rice by about 2cm/¾in.

4 Bring to the boil, reduce the heat to the lowest setting and stir the rice once. Cover the pan tightly and cook as gently as possible for 20 minutes.

5 Remove the pan from the heat and leave to stand, without uncovering the pan, for 15 minutes.

6 Arrange a portion of rice on each plate. Mould it neatly in a small ring or ramekin dish, if liked. Decorate the dish with the pine nuts and a dusting of cinnamon.

Per portion Energy 582kcal/2450kJ; Protein 9.5g; Carbohydrate 125.3g, of which sugars 44.5g; Fat 4.9g, of which saturates 0.5g; Cholesterol 0mg; Calcium 50mg; Fibre 1.4g; Sodium 13mg.

THREE-COLOUR RIBBON COOKIES

These delightful ribbon cookies, called maejakgwa, taste as good as they look. The crisp twists of wafer-thin dough are tinted in pastel shades of green, yellow and pink, and have a hint of ginger. They are perfect served with a sweet drink or a cup of green tea.

SERVES FOUR

INGREDIENTS
    30ml/2 tbsp pine nuts, finely ground
    vegetable oil, for deep-frying
For the green cookies
    115g/4oz/1 cup plain
      (all-purpose) flour
    2.5ml/½ tsp salt
    10g/¼oz grated fresh root ginger
    30ml/2 tbsp seaweed, finely ground
For the yellow cookies
    115g/4oz/1 cup plain
      (all-purpose) flour
    2.5ml/½ tsp salt
    10g/¼oz grated fresh root ginger
    50g/2oz sweet pumpkin, finely
      minced (ground)
For the pink cookies
    115g/4oz/1 cup plain
      (all-purpose) flour
    2.5ml/½ tsp salt
    10g/¼oz grated fresh root ginger
    50g/2oz apricot flesh, finely minced
      (ground)
For the syrup
    250ml/8fl oz/1 cup water
    200g/7oz/1 cup sugar
    30ml/2 tbsp honey
    2.5ml/½ tsp cinnamon
    salt

1 To make the green cookies, sift the flour and salt into a large bowl and mix in the grated ginger, ground seaweed and a splash of water. Knead gently into a smooth, elastic dough.

2 Place on a lightly floured surface and roll out the dough to about 3mm/⅛in thick. Cut the dough into strips 2cm/¾in wide and 5cm/2in long.

3 To make the yellow cookies, sift the flour and salt into a large bowl and mix in the grated ginger, minced pumpkin and a splash of water. Continue as for the green cookies, kneading the dough, rolling out and cutting into strips 2cm/¾in wide and 5cm/2in long.

4 To make the pink cookies, sift the flour and salt into a large bowl and mix in the grated ginger, minced apricot and a splash of water. Continue as for the green cookies.

5 Score three cuts lengthways into each cookie, and bring one end of the strip back through the centre slit to form a loose knot.

6 To make the cinnamon syrup, put the water, sugar and honey in a pan, and add a pinch of salt. Bring to the boil without stirring, then add the cinnamon and continue to boil, stirring until the syrup becomes sticky. Pour into a bowl.

7 Pour a generous amount of vegetable oil into a heavy pan, and heat over a medium heat to 150°C/300°F, or when a small piece of bread browns in about 20 seconds. Add the cookies and deep-fry until golden brown.

8 Drain the cookies on kitchen paper, then dip into the cinnamon syrup. Arrange on a serving plate and dust the cookies with the ground pine nuts before serving.

COOK'S TIPS
• Although getting the cookies to form the right shape can seem difficult at first, it will become much easier with practice. Don't lose heart.
• As an alternative to ingredients that colour the dough, you can use edible food colourings to introduce other colours and make them more appealing for children.

Per portion Energy 669kcal/2827kJ; Protein 9.7g; Carbohydrate 126.5g, of which sugars 60.7g; Fat 17.3g, of which saturates 1.8g; Cholesterol 0mg; Calcium 154mg; Fibre 3.2g; Sodium 498mg.

SWEET POTATO JELLY

*WHILE DESSERTS ARE UNCOMMON IN KOREA, THIS DELICATELY SWEET JELLY IS SOMETIMES SERVED
AFTER A MEAL. IT IS ALSO POPULAR AS A SNACK OR AS A LIGHT ACCOMPANIMENT TO AFTERNOON TEA.
THE MAPLE SYRUP GIVES IT A DISTINCTIVE UNDERTONE.*

SERVES TWO

INGREDIENTS
    2 small sweet potatoes
    60ml/4 tbsp maple syrup
    30ml/2 tbsp black sesame seeds
    15ml/1 tbsp powdered agar
    vegetable oil, for greasing mould

1 Peel the sweet potatoes and cut
them into chunks, then place them
in a pan. Add enough water to cover
and then bring to the boil over a
high heat. Reduce the heat slightly
and simmer the potatoes for
approximately 15 minutes, until
they are tender.

2 Drain and mash the potatoes until
completely smooth, then mix in the
maple syrup and sesame seeds. Bring
200ml/7fl oz/scant 1 cup water to
simmering point over a medium heat.
Add the agar and stir until dissolved.

3 Add the sweet potato to the pan and
stir well. Simmer for 5 minutes, stirring
frequently, and remove from the heat.

4 Grease a mould with a little oil. Pour
in the potato mixture and cool. Then
chill until the jelly has set.

5 Cover the mould with a board and
invert. Lift the mould off the jelly. Slice
and arrange on a shallow dish to serve.

Per portion Energy 310kcal/1309kJ; Protein 4.6g; Carbohydrate 55.8g, of which sugars 32.3g; Fat 9.2g, of which saturates 1.4g; Cholesterol 0mg; Calcium 142mg; Fibre 4.8g; Sodium 144mg.

FLOWER PETAL RICE CAKES <u>IN</u> HONEY

THIS GORGEOUS SPRING DISH, CALLED HWACHUN, USES EDIBLE FLOWER PETALS TO FLAVOUR RICE CAKES, WHICH ARE THEN DRIZZLED WITH HONEY. ITS SOPHISTICATED APPEARANCE IS MATCHED BY ITS REFINED, EXQUISITE TASTE. SERVE WITH A CUP OF GREEN TEA.

SERVES FOUR

INGREDIENTS
20 edible flower petals
225g/8oz/2 cups sweet
  rice flour
2.5ml/½ tsp salt
vegetable oil, for shallow-frying
honey, for drizzling

1 Rinse the flower petals, and gently pat them dry with kitchen paper.

2 Sift the flour and salt into a bowl and add 300ml/½ pint/1¼ cups of warm water. Mix well and knead for 10 minutes. Place on a lightly floured surface and roll out the dough to 1cm/½in thick. Use a floured 5cm/2in biscuit (cookie) cutter to cut the dough into rounds.

3 Heat the oil in a frying pan over a low flame. Add the rice cakes and fry for 2 minutes, or until lightly browned. Flip over and cook on the other side, and then remove from the pan. Place on kitchen paper to blot the excess oil, then arrange on a serving platter.

4 Sprinkle the petals over the rice cakes, and then drizzle with honey.

COOK'S TIPS
• A number of different flowers have edible petals, including roses, azaleas, apple blossom, carnations and chrysanthemums, and they can sometimes be found at supermarkets or grocery stores.
• If you have food or pollen allergies, check with your doctor before consuming flower petals to avoid any adverse reaction.
• Do not eat petals from flowers that have been sprayed with pesticides, so either grow your own, or check the growing conditions with the supplier.

Per portion Energy 255kcal/1065kJ; Protein 3.6g; Carbohydrate 45.1g, of which sugars 0g; Fat 6g, of which saturates 0.7g; Cholesterol 0mg; Calcium 14mg; Fibre 1.1g; Sodium 249mg.

PERSIMMON AND WALNUT PUNCH

THIS NON-ALCOHOLIC PUNCH IS A POPULAR DESSERT IN KOREA. THE SWEETNESS OF THE DRIED PERSIMMONS IS MATCHED BY THE SHARPNESS OF THE CINNAMON, AND THE DISH HAS A REFRESHING FRUITY KICK THAT EFFECTIVELY BALANCES OUT A SPICY MAIN MEAL.

SERVES FOUR

INGREDIENTS
    12 dried persimmons
    12 walnuts
    150g/5oz fresh root ginger, peeled
      and thinly sliced
    1 cinnamon stick/½ tsp ground
      cinnamon
    450g/1lb/2 cups light muscovado
      (brown) sugar
    30ml/2 tbsp maple syrup or golden
      (light corn) syrup
    30 pine nuts

1 Seed the dried persimmons and soak them in cold water until they have softened. Then make an incision into the centre of each, and stuff each one with a walnut. Set aside.

2 Pour 1 litre/1¾ pints/4 cups water into a pan and add the ginger and cinnamon stick or powder. Place over a low heat and simmer gently for 15 minutes, or until the water has taken on the flavour of the ginger and cinnamon.

3 When the liquid has reduced by about a fifth to a quarter, strain it through muslin (cheesecloth) into a large jug (pitcher).

4 Pour the liquid back into the pan, add the sugar and maple or golden syrup and then bring the contents to the boil again.

5 Remove the pan from the heat and pour the punch into a jug. Cool, then chill in the refrigerator.

6 Place three persimmons in a small serving bowl for each person, and then pour over the chilled liquid. Decorate each bowl with a sprinkling of pine nuts, and serve.

Per portion Energy 379kcal/1589kJ; Protein 4.9g; Carbohydrate 48.4g, of which sugars 48.3g; Fat 19.8g, of which saturates 1.6g; Cholesterol 0mg; Calcium 47mg; Fibre 1.6g; Sodium 31mg.

INDEX

Above: Pumpkin congee is a naturally sweet dessert or snack.

PUBLISHER'S ACKNOWLEDGEMENTS

The publishers would like to thank the following for permission to
reproduce their images: t = top; b = bottom; r = right
8t Chad Ehlers/Alamy; p8b YONHAP/epa/Corbis; p9t LOOK Die
Bildagentur der Fotografen GmbH/Alamy; p9b Carl and Ann
Purcell/Corbis; p10t Christophe Boisvieux/Corbis; p10b Kim Kyung-
Hoon/Reuters/Corbis; p11t istock; p11b Michel Setboun/Corbis;
p12t Michael Freeman/Corbis; p12br Bob Krist/Corbis; p13 Tropix

Photo Library; p14 Michael Setboun/Corbis; p14b and p15t Tropix
Photo Library; p15b Horizon International Images Limited/Alamy;
All other photographs © Anness Publishing.

With grateful thanks to Ran Restaurant at 58–59 Great
Marlborough Street, London for their help with photographing
equipment. Also to Veronica Birley of Tropix Photo Library for her trip
to Korea with our project in mind.